EDITOR: Maryanne Blacker
FOOD EDITOR: Pamela Clark
■ ■ ■
ASSISTANT FOOD EDITOR: Jan Castorina
ASSISTANT EDITOR: Bridget van Tinteren
ART DIRECTOR: Sue de Guingand
DESIGNER: Robbylee Phelan
EDITORIAL COORDINATOR: Fiona Lambrou
■ ■ ■
ACP PUBLISHER: Richard Walsh
ACP DEPUTY PUBLISHER: Nick Chan
■ ■ ■

Produced by The Australian Women's Weekly Home Library.
Typeset by ACP Color Graphics Pty Ltd.
Printed by Times Printers Pte. Ltd, Singapore.
Published by ACP Publishing Pty Ltd, 54 Park Street, Sydney.

♦ U.S.A.: Distributed for Whitecap Books Ltd by
Graphic Arts Center Publishing, 3019 N.W. Yeon,
Portland, OR, 97210. Tel: 503-226-2402. Fax: 530-223-1410.

♦ CANADA: Distributed in Canada by Whitecap
Books Ltd, 1086 West 3rd St,
North Vancouver BC V7P 3J6. Tel: 604- 980-9852.
Fax: 604-980-8197.

■ ■ ■

Italian Cooking Class Cookbook
Includes index.
ISBN 1 86396 013 9

■ ■ ■

■ ■ ■

COVER: Fish Soup, page 16; Antipasto, page 2;
Vegetable Salad, page 84; Mamma's Cake, page 96;
Florentines, page 98.
OPPOSITE: Tortellini, page 40.
INSIDE BACK COVER: Pizza, page 56.

Italian
COOKING CLASS COOKBOOK

W9-CDG-108

In Italy, dishes vary according to the region.
In this book, former Food Editor Ellen Sinclair, has drawn
recipes from all regions and the wide range represents
Italian cooking at its best.

Pamela Clark
FOOD EDITOR

ANTIPASTO

Antipasto makes a light and tempting start to a meal. It can be a colorful array from a delicatessen, as shown in the photograph at right: prosciutto, mortadella, an assortment of salamis and cold meats, olives, artichoke hearts, slices of fresh cantaloupe, plus marinated button mushrooms.

On the following pages, we offer other ideas; choose a variety of dishes and put a tablespoon or so of each on a serving platter. Quantities for each give 4 to 6 servings.

EGGPLANT APPETIZER
Antipasto di Melanzane

YOU WILL NEED
2 large eggplants
1 cup olive oil
¼ cup olive oil, extra
3 cloves garlic, minced
**3 ripe tomatoes, peeled,
    seeded, chopped**
4 teaspoons tomato paste
½ cup water

1. Cut unpeeled eggplant lengthways into ¼ inch slices. Cut slices into 2½ inch lengths.

2. Heat oil in skillet, add half the eggplant, cook, stirring gently, about 5 minutes or until eggplant is soft. Remove from skillet with slotted spoon; drain on absorbent paper. Repeat with remaining eggplant.

Heat extra oil in skillet, add garlic, tomatoes, paste and water. Simmer, uncovered, about 10 minutes or until sauce is thick. Add eggplant, stir lightly to combine.

Note: *Recipe can be made 2 days ahead. Serve hot or cold. Not suitable to freeze.*

VEGETABLE PICKLES

YOU WILL NEED
¼ cauliflower
2 carrots
6 pearl onions
1 red bell pepper
1 cucumber
**2½ cups red or white
    wine vinegar**
12 black peppercorns
2 teaspoons mustard seeds

*There are three methods used to
sterilize jars.
1. Place jars in dishwasher, use
rinse cycle and hottest temperature;
do not add detergent.
2. Place clean jars in a large pan,
cover with cold water, cover pan,
bring to boil; boil 20 minutes.
Remove jars from water; drain
well, stand right way up on a clean
wooden board.
3. Wash jars well in hot soapy
water, rinse thoroughly in hot
water. Stand jars right
way up on baking sheet, place in
300°F oven 30 minutes.*

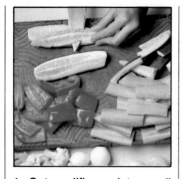

1. Cut cauliflower into small florets. Cut carrots lengthways into thick slices, halve slices crossways. Peel onions. Cut pepper into large pieces. Cut cucumber lengthways into quarters, remove seeds, cut each quarter in half lengthways then in half crossways.

2. Cook all vegetables in pan of boiling salted water 2 minutes; drain. Pack vegetables into a hot sterilized jar.

3. Combine vinegar, pepper-corns and seeds in pan, bring to boil. Pour over vegetables to cover completely; seal while hot. Cool; refrigerate at least 1 week before using.

Makes about 6 cups.

Note: *Recipe can be made
1 month ahead; keep refrigerated.
Not suitable to freeze.*

MARINATED MUSHROOMS

Funghi Marinati

YOU WILL NEED
½lb button mushrooms
¼ cup fresh lemon juice
½ cup olive oil
**3 tablespoons chopped
    fresh parsley**
**¼ teaspoon dried tarragon
    leaves**
**¼ teaspoon ground black
    pepper**

1. Wash mushrooms, remove stalks, slice mushrooms thinly.

2. Combine juice, oil, parsley, tarragon and pepper in bowl; mix well. Add mushrooms; mix well. Cover, refrigerate mixture 4 hours or overnight.

Marinated mushrooms are also delicious tossed in a green salad. Remove mushrooms from marinade with slotted spoon, add to salad greens; add enough of the marinade to coat salad greens lightly; toss well.

Note: *Recipe can be made 2 days
ahead. Not suitable to freeze.*

4

BEANS WITH TOMATO
Fagioli al Pomodoro

YOU WILL NEED
2lb fresh white beans
2 onions
3 ripe tomatoes
2oz can anchovies
2 tablespoons (¼ stick)
    butter
1 clove garlic, minced
2 tablespoons tomato paste
1 teaspoon dried basil leaves
½ teaspoon sugar
1 cup water

1. Shell beans, discard pods.

2. Finely chop onions. Peel and chop tomatoes. Drain and finely chop anchovies.

3. Melt butter in pan, add garlic, onions, tomatoes and anchovies, cook, stirring, until onion is soft. Stir in beans, paste, basil, sugar and water. Simmer, covered, about 30 minutes or until beans are tender.

Note: *Recipe can be made a day ahead. Reheat just before serving. Not suitable to freeze. When white beans are out of season, 10oz canned red beans or white kidney beans (cannellini) can be substituted. Drain and rinse beans, add for last 10 minutes of cooking.*

SICILIAN CAPONATA
Caponata alla Siciliana

YOU WILL NEED
1 eggplant
coarse (kosher) salt
¼ cup olive oil
1 onion, chopped
2 red bell peppers, chopped
1 stalk celery, sliced
14½oz can tomatoes
3 tablespoons brown vinegar
4 teaspoons sugar
1 clove garlic, minced
8 pitted black olives, sliced
4 teaspoons drained capers

1. Cut eggplant into ½ inch cubes, place in colander, sprinkle with salt, stand 1 hour. Rinse well, pat dry with absorbent paper. Heat oil in large skillet, add onion, peppers and celery, cook, stirring, 5 minutes.

2. Add eggplant, cook, stirring, further 5 minutes. Sieve undrained tomatoes into skillet; discard seeds.

3. Add vinegar, sugar and garlic, cook, stirring, further 2 minutes. Stir in olives and capers, simmer, uncovered, about 15 minutes or until most of the liquid has been evaporated.

Note: *Recipe can be made a day ahead. Reheat just before serving. Not suitable to freeze. This dish also makes an excellent vegetable accompaniment to main courses.*

BELL PEPPER RELISH

Condimento al Pepe

YOU WILL NEED
3 green bell peppers
3 onions
3 ripe tomatoes
3 tablespoons olive oil
½ cup white vinegar

1. Remove seeds from peppers, slice peppers lengthways. Peel and slice onions. Peel and chop tomatoes.

2. Place peppers, onions, tomatoes and oil in large pan. Simmer, covered, 1 hour, stirring occasionally.

3. Add vinegar, simmer, uncovered, 15 minutes. Place in bowl or in jar, cover; refrigerate until cold.

Note: *Recipe can be made 3 days ahead. Serve cold. Not suitable to freeze.*

GLAZED ONIONS

Cipolle Glassate

YOU WILL NEED
1lb pearl onions
¼ cup olive oil
¼ cup white vinegar
2 tablespoons superfine sugar
4 whole cloves
1 bay leaf

1. Place unpeeled onions in bowl, cover with boiling water, stand 5 minutes.

2. Drain onions. Using a small sharp knife, peel onions, taking care to leave ends intact so onions do not fall apart.

3. Combine oil, vinegar, sugar, cloves and bay leaf in pan. Add onions, simmer gently, covered, about 20 minutes or until onions are tender and sauce becomes syrupy in consistency.

Note: *Recipe can be made 2 days ahead. Serve hot or cold. Not suitable to freeze.*

SOUPS

Italian soups can be clear and light or thick and hearty but, whatever the type, good flavor is all-important.

MINESTRONE

YOU WILL NEED
3 carrots
3 stalks celery
2 onions
½lb potatoes
2 zucchini
3oz green beans
½ cup olive oil
3 tablespoons butter
½lb cabbage, shredded
5 cups beef broth
28oz can tomatoes
10oz canned white kidney beans (cannellini)

2. Heat oil and butter in large pan, add onions, cook, stirring, until pale golden brown. Add carrots, cook, stirring, about 3 minutes or until almost tender.

1. Finely chop carrots, celery, onions, potatoes, zucchini and beans separately.

3. Repeat cooking with potatoes, then celery, zucchini, beans and cabbage. Stir in broth and undrained crushed tomatoes. Simmer, covered, 1½ hours. Stir in rinsed and drained beans, simmer, covered, further 15 minutes or until soup is thick.

Serves 4 to 6.

Note: *Recipe can be made 2 days ahead. Reheat just before serving. Not suitable to freeze. Grated Parmesan cheese can be served with the minestrone, if desired.*

STRACCIATELLA

YOU WILL NEED
2 chicken thighs, skinned
1 carrot, chopped
1 onion, chopped
1 stalk celery, chopped
6 cups water
1 teaspoon black
**   peppercorns**
2 eggs
¾ cup grated fresh
**   Parmesan cheese**
3 tablespoons chopped
**   fresh parsley**
ground black pepper

1. Place chicken, vegetables, water and peppercorns in large pan, simmer, covered, 1 hour.

2. Strain broth through sieve into another pan. Discard chicken and vegetables; only the broth is required in this soup. (Chicken and vegetables can be used for another meal.)

3. Skim a clean, piece of absorbent paper over surface of hot broth to remove any fat. Repeat two or three times, using fresh paper. (Alternatively, cool broth, refrigerate until cold; remove fat from surface.)

4. Beat eggs, cheese and parsley together in jug or bowl. Bring broth to boil in pan. While stirring broth vigorously with one hand, add egg mixture gradually in a thin stream with the other. Continue stirring over heat 1 to 2 minutes after all egg mixture has been added, remove mixture from heat immediately. Season with pepper.
Serves 4 to 6.

Note: Broth can be made 4 days ahead. Soup best made just before serving. Broth suitable to freeze.

MEATBALL SOUP *Brodo con Polpettine di Carne*

YOU WILL NEED
1½lb beef bones
2 carrots
2 stalks celery
14½oz can tomatoes
½ cup small dried pasta
4 teaspoons chopped fresh
**   parsley**
MEATBALLS
1lb ground beef
1 egg
½ cup fresh bread crumbs

1. Place beef bones, carrots and celery in large pan, cover with cold water, simmer, covered, 1 hour. Skim any fat from soup while it is cooking.

2. Remove celery and carrots from broth, cool; chop. Remove bones from broth, strain broth into large bowl; return to pan. Add carrots, celery and undrained crushed tomatoes, simmer, covered, 15 minutes.

3. Add pasta to pan of boiling water, boil, uncovered, until just tender; drain. Add pasta to soup with meatballs, simmer further 10 minutes; stir in parsley.

Meatballs: Combine beef, egg and bread crumbs in bowl; mix well. Roll heaped teaspoons of mixture into balls. Place in small greased roasting pan in single layer. Bake meatballs, covered, in 350˚F oven 45 minutes, turning occasionally. Remove, drain on absorbent paper.
Serves 6.

Note: Broth can be made 4 days ahead. Meatballs can be made a day ahead. Soup best made just before serving. Broth and meatballs suitable to freeze.

BACCALA SOUP *Zuppa di Baccala*

YOU WILL NEED
14oz packaged baccala fillets
¼ cup light olive oil
2 cloves garlic, minced
2 onions, thinly sliced
1 stalk celery, finely chopped
**¼ teaspoon dried thyme
    leaves**
**4 teaspoons chopped fresh
    parsley**
14½oz can tomatoes
¼ cup dry white wine
4 cups water
2 potatoes, chopped
**4 teaspoons chopped fresh
    parsley, extra**
**¼ teaspoon ground black
    pepper**

Baccala is dried, salted cod, imported from Norway.

Fillets of baccala come in packaged form and these are easier to cook because they contain fewer bones. They are available from delicatessens.

Baccala should be put into a large bowl of water and left in the refrigerator for 36 hours to soften the fish and remove excess salt; change the water often during soaking time.

Zuppa di Baccala is one of the most popular soups in both northern and southern Italy.

1. Soak baccala in large bowl of water for 36 hours, changing water frequently. Drain well, dry thoroughly with absorbent paper. Cut baccala into pieces, removing as many bones and as much skin as possible (or remove during cooking time).

2. Heat oil in large pan, add garlic and onions, cook, stirring, over low heat until golden but not browned. Add celery, thyme and parsley, cook, stirring, 3 minutes.

3. Sieve undrained tomatoes into pan; discard seeds. Simmer, covered, 10 minutes.

4. Add wine, water and potatoes to pan.

5. Add baccala, simmer gently, uncovered, 1 hour. Stir in extra parsley and pepper.
Serves 4.

Note: *Recipe can be made a day ahead. Reheat just before serving. Not suitable to freeze.*

MUSSEL SOUP

Zuppa di Cozze

YOU WILL NEED
24 mussels
1lb white fish fillets
6 cups water
1 stalk celery, chopped
1 onion, chopped
1 carrot, chopped
2 tablespoons (¼ stick) butter
¼ cup all-purpose flour
2 teaspoons curry powder
3 tablespoons tomato paste
2 chicken bouillon cubes
2 tomatoes, peeled, chopped
¼ teaspoon ground black pepper
3 tablespoons chopped fresh parsley

1. Clean mussels by scrubbing them with a brush under cold running water. Remove beard – the hairy substance around each – by pulling.

2. Skin and bone fish, cut fish into large portions. Combine fish, water and vegetables in large pan, simmer, covered, 15 minutes.

3. Drain mixture, reserve broth and fish; discard vegetables. Melt butter in pan, add flour and curry powder, cook, stirring, 1 minute. Remove from heat, gradually add combined paste and fish broth. Stir over heat until soup boils and thickens. Add crumbled bouillon cubes, tomatoes and pepper; simmer 1 minute.

4. Add mussels and flaked fish, simmer further 5 minutes or until mussels have opened. Stir in chopped parsley.

Serves 6.

Note: Recipe best made close to serving. Broth can be made several hours ahead. Broth suitable to freeze.

FISH SOUP

Zuppa di Pesce

YOU WILL NEED
4 fish fillets
2 onions, sliced
few sprigs parsley
1 stalk celery, chopped
5 cups water
1 cup dry white wine
½lb cooked shrimp
½lb mussels
½lb baby clams
14½oz can tomatoes
1lb fish fillets, extra
2 ripe tomatoes, peeled, seeded, chopped
2 potatoes, chopped
1 clove garlic, minced
1 teaspoon dried oregano leaves
½ teaspoon sugar
4 teaspoons tomato paste
¼ teaspoon ground black pepper
3 tablespoons chopped fresh parsley

1. Combine the 4 fish fillets, onions, parsley, celery, water and wine in large pan, simmer, covered, 30 minutes. Strain broth through fine sieve, return broth to pan, discard vegetables. Flake fish and reserve.

Shell and devein shrimp. Scrub mussels; remove beards. Scrub clams. Place mussels and clams in large pan of boiling water, boil, covered, until shells open; remove immediately from water.

2. Sieve undrained canned tomatoes; discard seeds. Remove skin and any bones from extra fish, chop fish. Add canned and chopped tomatoes, fish, potatoes, garlic, oregano, sugar, paste and pepper to broth. Simmer, covered, further 30 minutes.

4. Add shrimp and reserved fish to soup, bring to boil, add parsley, mussels and clams, simmer until heated through.

Serves 6.

Note: Recipe best made close to serving. Broth can be made 6 hours ahead. Broth suitable to freeze.

CLAM SOUP

YOU WILL NEED
2 fish fillets
½ onion, sliced
1 green onion, chopped
3½ cups water
2lb baby clams
3 tablespoons light olive oil
5 green onions, finely chopped, extra
6oz button mushrooms, sliced
½ cup milk
4 teaspoons cornstarch
¼ cup dry white wine
¼ teaspoon ground white pepper

1. Remove skin and bones from fish. Combine fish, onion, green onion and water in pan, simmer, covered, 15 minutes. Drain; reserve broth and fish separately.

2. Soak clams in cold salted water 10 minutes. Scrub clams, rinse well; drain. Place clams in pan, cover and shake over high heat until clams open. Remove opened clams during cooking until all clams have opened. Drain and reserve liquid in pan. Remove half the clams from their shells, leaving remaining clams intact.

3. Heat oil in pan, add extra green onions and mushrooms, cook, stirring, until mushrooms are soft.

4. Add reserved broth, reserved clam liquid and milk, bring to boil, stir in blended cornstarch and wine, stir until mixture boils. Add flaked fish, all the clams and pepper; simmer until heated through.
Serves 4

Note: Recipe best made just before serving. Broth can be made 6 hours ahead. Broth suitable to freeze. If unable to buy fresh clams, substitute 10oz canned clams. Drain clams, add to soup at end of cooking time to heat

BEAN AND PASTA SOUP

YOU WILL NEED
½lb white kidney beans (cannellini)
6 cups water
¼lb bacon pieces
3 tablespoons light olive oil
1 onion, finely chopped
1 stalk celery, finely chopped
2 cloves garlic, minced
½lb bacon bones
¾ cup small dried pasta
2 tablespoons chopped fresh parsley
¼ teaspoon ground white pepper

1. Combine beans and water in large pan, bring to boil, boil, covered, 2 minutes. Remove from heat, stand, covered, 1 hour. Do not drain. Trim rind from bacon pieces, chop bacon finely. Heat oil in large pan, add bacon, vegetables and garlic, cook, stirring, until browned. Add bacon bones with bacon and vegetable mixture to beans, simmer, covered, 1 to 1½ hours or until beans are tender.

2. Remove bacon bones from soup, remove any meat from bones; discard bones, finely chop meat. Using slotted spoon, remove about half the cooked beans from the soup, blend or process until smooth. (Meat from bacon bones can also be processed or blended with the beans.) Skim any fat from surface of soup. Return bean mixture to soup; simmer gently while pasta is cooking.

3. Add pasta to pan of boiling water, boil, uncovered, until just tender; drain. Add pasta to soup with parsley and pepper.
Serves 6.

Note: Recipe can be prepared 2 days ahead. Cook pasta and add to reheated soup just before serving. Add extra water to soup, if necessary. Not suitable to freeze. Bacon pieces, onion and celery can be finely chopped in a food processor.

BRODO

YOU WILL NEED
1lb boned beef shank
2 chicken thighs, skinned
1 stalk celery
1 onion
1 small potato
½ green bell pepper
1 carrot
1 veal shank, sliced

1. Remove any excess fat from beef and chicken. Cut beef into small pieces. Chop celery, quarter onion, peel potato, roughly chop pepper and quarter carrot lengthways. Combine all ingredients in large pan, add cold water to cover. Cook, partially covered, over high heat until boiling. Simmer, covered, skimming foam from surface frequently, 3 hours.

2. Remove beef, chicken and veal; reserve for another meal. Strain broth through large strainer lined with cheesecloth or clean kitchen towel; discard vegetable mixture. Cool, cover, refrigerate several hours or overnight; remove fat from broth. Bring broth to boil just before serving.

Makes about 4 cups.

Note: *Recipe can be made 3 days ahead. Suitable to freeze. Ask your butcher to slice the veal shank for you. Brodo – a light, clear broth – can be eaten by itself or have cooked tortellini, cooked pasta or thinly sliced cooked vegetables added. If you want a good, hearty soup, the meat and chicken can be returned to the soup with chopped parsley.*

LENTIL SOUP

Minestra di Lenticchie

YOU WILL NEED
1 onion
1 carrot
1 stalk celery
1 tablespoon butter
2 tablespoons light olive oil
½lb bacon bones
½lb brown lentils
14½oz can tomatoes
4 cups water
2 beef bouillon cubes
¼ teaspoon ground black
**   pepper**
3 tablespoons chopped
**   fresh parsley**

1. Chop onion, carrot and celery.

2. Heat butter and oil in pan, add onion, carrot and celery, cook, stirring, until onion is soft. Add bacon bones, lentils, undrained crushed tomatoes, water and crumbled bouillon cubes. Simmer, covered, about 1½ hours or until lentils are tender. Remove and discard bacon bones; add pepper and parsley.

Serves 4.

Note: *Recipe can be made 2 days ahead. Reheat just before serving. Suitable to freeze. Bacon bones are very salty, so there is no need to add extra salt to this recipe.*

SAUCES FOR PASTA

Spoon these sauces over any favorite pasta: spaghetti, fettuccine, tagliatelle, macaroni and more.

SICILIANA

YOU WILL NEED
1 small eggplant
1 small green bell pepper
2oz can anchovies
milk
10 pitted black olives
4 teaspoons capers
1/3 cup olive oil
1 onion, grated
2 cloves garlic, minced
28oz can tomatoes
1/2 teaspoon dried basil
   leaves (or 1 teaspoon
   chopped fresh basil)
1/4 cup chopped fresh
   parsley
1/4 teaspoon ground
   black pepper

Peel and chop eggplant; chop pepper. Drain anchovies, cover with milk in bowl, stand 10 minutes; drain anchovies well (this removes excess salt). Finely chop anchovies, olives and capers.

Heat oil in pan, add eggplant, pepper and onion, cook, stirring, until eggplant is soft. Add garlic, undrained crushed tomatoes and basil, simmer, covered, 30 minutes.

Add anchovies, olives, capers, parsley and black pepper, simmer, covered, further 5 minutes.

Serves 4 to 6.

Note: Recipe can be made a day ahead. Reheat just before serving. Not suitable to freeze.

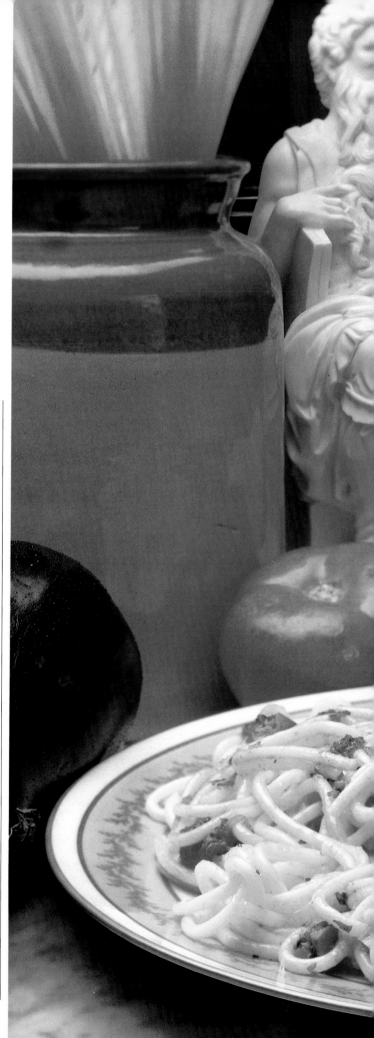

SEAFOOD

YOU WILL NEED
¼lb sea scallops
1lb cooked shrimp
¼ cup (½ stick) butter
2 cloves garlic, minced
½ cup dry white wine
1¼ cups heavy cream
4 teaspoons arrowroot or
cornstarch
¼ cup water
1 teaspoon fresh lemon juice
4 teaspoons chopped fresh
parsley
3 green onions, chopped
8 oysters in half shells

1. Clean scallops and separate coral (as in picture); cut scallops in half. Shell, devein and coarsely chop shrimp.

2. Melt butter in skillet, add garlic, cook, stirring, until fragrant. Add wine and cream, bring to boil, boil, uncovered, 4 minutes. Stir in blended arrowroot and water, stir until mixture boils. Add scallops, shrimp and juice, simmer 2 minutes or until scallops are just cooked. Stir in parsley and onions. Garnish with oysters drizzled with a little of the sauce.

Serves 4.

Note: Recipe best made just before serving. Not suitable to freeze. Half-and-half can be used in place of heavy cream, if preferred.

PESTO

YOU WILL NEED
3 bunches fresh basil
4 teaspoons olive oil
3 tablespoons pine nuts
2 cloves garlic, minced
ground black pepper
¼ cup olive oil, extra
¼ cup grated fresh
Parmesan cheese

1. Wash basil, remove leaves from stems, discard stems. (You will need about 2 cups of leaves.)

2. Combine oil and nuts in small pan, cook, stirring, over low heat until nuts are lightly browned; drain immediately.

3. Process basil, nuts, garlic and pepper until finely chopped and smooth. With motor operating, add extra oil in a thin stream. Process further 1 second. (Blender can also be used; stop blender and scrape down mixture occasionally.)

4. Transfer mixture to bowl, add cheese; mix well.

Serves 4 to 6.

Note: Recipe can be made a week ahead. Spoon into jar, cover pesto with olive oil, top with lid; keep refrigerated. Suitable to freeze without cheese.

PESCATORE

YOU WILL NEED
1lb mussels
3oz crabmeat
2 ripe tomatoes, peeled
½ green bell pepper
1lb fish fillets
28oz can tomatoes
3 tablespoons olive oil
¼ cup dry white wine

1. Scrub mussels, remove beards. Add mussels to pan of boiling water, boil about 3 minutes or until mussels open; drain. Remove mussel meat from shells.

2. Flake crabmeat. Chop ripe tomatoes; finely chop pepper. Skin and bone fish, cut into ½ inch pieces. Sieve undrained canned tomatoes into bowl; discard seeds.

3. Heat oil in skillet, add fish, cook, stirring gently, until lightly browned. Add chopped tomato, pepper, sieved tomatoes and wine, simmer, uncovered, 10 minutes, stirring occasionally. Add crabmeat and mussel meat, simmer until sauce is heated through.

Serves 6.

Note: Recipe best made just before serving. Not suitable to freeze.

CHICKEN LIVERS

Fegatini di Pollo

YOU WILL NEED
½lb chicken livers
¼ cup olive oil
2 onions, chopped
⅔ cup heavy cream
2 eggs, lightly beaten
grated fresh Parmesan
    cheese

1. Wash, trim and chop livers. Heat oil in skillet, add onions, cook, stirring, until lightly browned. Add livers, cook until they just change color.

2. Add cream; mix well. Simmer, uncovered, 2 minutes. Quickly stir in eggs; remove from heat immediately. Serve topped with Parmesan cheese.

Serves 2.

Note: Recipe best made just before serving. Not suitable to freeze. Half and half can be used in place of heavy cream, if preferred.

MARINARA

YOU WILL NEED
1lb shrimp
½lb sea scallops
2oz can anchovies
8 oysters
½ cup water
½ cup dry white wine
3 tablespoons olive oil
5 large ripe tomatoes,
    peeled, chopped
2 cloves garlic, minced
4 teaspoons tomato paste
4 teaspoons chopped
    fresh parsley
4 teaspoons chopped
    fresh mint
ground black pepper

1. Shell and devein shrimp; cut scallops in half. Drain anchovies on absorbent paper; chop finely. Carefully remove oysters from shells.

2. Combine water and wine in skillet, add scallops, cook 1 minute; drain. Heat oil in skillet, add tomatoes, garlic and paste, stir until combined, simmer, uncovered, 2 minutes. Add seafood, simmer further minute. Stir in parsley, mint and pepper.

Serves 4.

Note: *Recipe best made just before serving. Not suitable to freeze. Any type of shellfish can be used in this recipe.*

TOMATO SAUCES *Salse di Pomodoro*

Here are two of the most popular light tomato sauces for pasta. They are excellent for vegetarian meals.

NEAPOLITAN SAUCE *Salsa di Pomodoro alla Napoletana*

YOU WILL NEED
2 tablespoons (¼ stick)
    butter
4 teaspoons olive oil
28oz can tomatoes
½ teaspoon dried basil
    leaves
3 tablespoons chopped
    fresh parsley

Heat butter and oil in skillet. Sieve undrained tomatoes into skillet; discard seeds. Stir in basil, simmer, uncovered, about 30 minutes or until sauce is reduced by about half. Stir in parsley just before serving.

Serves 2.

Note: *Recipe can be made a day ahead. Reheat just before serving. Suitable to freeze.*

PIZZAIOLA *Alla Pizzaiola*

YOU WILL NEED
4 teaspoons olive oil
1 large clove garlic
28oz can tomatoes
¼ teaspoon dried marjoram
    leaves
3 tablespoons chopped
    fresh parsley

Heat oil in skillet, add garlic, cook, stirring, until lightly browned; discard garlic. Sieve undrained tomatoes into skillet; discard seeds. Stir in marjoram, simmer, uncovered, about 30 minutes or until sauce is reduced by about half. Stir in parsley just before serving.

Serves 2.

Note: *Recipe can be made a day ahead. Reheat just before serving. Suitable to freeze.*

TUNA & MUSHROOM

Tonno e Funghi

YOU WILL NEED
3oz (¾ stick) butter
1 large onion, finely chopped
2 x 7½oz cans tuna,
**   drained, flaked**
3oz button mushrooms,
**   halved**
1¼ cups heavy cream
3 tablespoons tomato paste
⅛ teaspoon ground
**   black pepper**
4 teaspoons chopped
**   fresh parsley**

Melt butter in skillet, add onion and tuna, cook, stirring, until onion is soft. Add mushrooms, cream, paste and pepper, bring to boil, remove from heat immediately; stir in parsley.

Serves 4.

Note: *Recipe best made just before serving. Not suitable to freeze. If preferred, 15oz fresh tuna can be used in place of canned tuna. Poach or broil tuna, cut into cubes.*

OIL & GARLIC

Aglio ed Olio

YOU WILL NEED
⅓ cup olive oil
3 cloves garlic, minced
3 tablespoons chopped
**   fresh parsley**
ground black pepper

Heat oil in skillet, add garlic, cook gently until lightly browned. Stir in chopped parsley and pepper.

Serves 4.

Note: *Recipe best made just before serving. Not suitable to freeze. A mixture of chopped fresh herbs can be used in place of parsley, if preferred.*

SUMMER

YOU WILL NEED
**1lb firm, ripe tomatoes,
 finely chopped
1 onion, chopped
6 pitted green olives,
 finely chopped
4 teaspoons capers,
 finely chopped
2 cloves garlic, minced
¼ teaspoon dried oregano
 leaves
⅓ cup chopped fresh
 parsley
½ cup olive oil**

Combine all ingredients in bowl; mix well. Cover, refrigerate overnight. Toss through hot pasta before serving.

Serves 4.

Note: *Recipe best made a day ahead. Use only ripe tomatoes in season for the best flavor. Bring mixture to room temperature before serving. Not suitable to freeze.*

MATRICIANA

YOU WILL NEED
**6 slices lean bacon
2 tablespoons olive oil
1 onion, finely chopped
1lb ripe tomatoes, peeled,
 seeded, chopped
1 fresh red chili pepper,
 seeded, finely chopped**

Remove rind from bacon, cut bacon crossways into thin strips. Heat oil in skillet, add bacon and onion, cook, stirring, until onion is soft; drain away excess fat. Add tomatoes and chili pepper; mix well. Simmer gently, uncovered, 5 minutes, stirring mixture occasionally.

Serves 4.

Note: *Recipe can be made a day ahead. Reheat just before serving. Not suitable to freeze. Serve with grated Parmesan or pecorino cheese, if desired. Pancetta – Italian salted pork – can be substituted for the bacon. It is available from most Italian delicatessens.*

ALFREDO

Salsa all' Alfredo

YOU WILL NEED
3oz (¾ stick) butter
⅔ cup heavy cream
1 cup grated fresh
   Parmesan cheese
chopped fresh parsley

Combine butter and cream in skillet, stir over low heat until butter is melted and well combined with cream. Remove from heat. Add cheese, stir until sauce is blended and smooth. Serve sprinkled with parsley.

Serves 4.

Note: Recipe best made just before serving. Not suitable to freeze. This sauce is traditionally served with fettuccine or tagliatelle.

CARBONARA

YOU WILL NEED
4 slices bacon or pancetta
⅓ cup heavy cream
⅛ teaspoon paprika
1 egg
1 egg yolk, extra
¾ cup grated fresh
   Parmesan cheese
½lb dried fettuccine or
   tagliatelle noodles
2 tablespoons (¼ stick)
   butter
ground black pepper

1. Remove rind from bacon, cut bacon into thin strips. Gently cook bacon in skillet until crisp. Drain all but 2 tablespoons of fat from skillet. Add cream and paprika, stir until combined.

2. Beat egg, extra egg yolk and half the cheese in bowl until combined. Add fettuccine to large pan of boiling water, boil, uncovered, until just tender. Drain, return fettuccine to pan with butter, toss over low heat until combined.

3. Add bacon mixture, toss well. Add egg mixture, toss until combined. Season with pepper. Serve sprinkled with remaining Parmesan cheese.

Serves 4 to 6.

Note: Recipe best made just before serving. Not suitable to freeze.

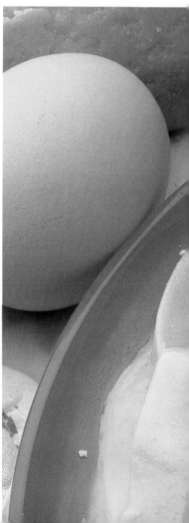

SPINACH WITH SPIRALI

Spirali e Spinaci

YOU WILL NEED
**8 leaves spinach or
  Swiss chard
¼ red bell pepper
3oz coppa
½ small onion
1 small fresh red chili pepper
⅓ cup olive oil
1 small clove garlic, minced
3 tablespoons grated fresh
  Parmesan cheese
ground black pepper**

1. Wash spinach, remove stalks, shred leaves finely. Finely chop bell pepper and coppa. Slice onion. Remove seeds from chili pepper, cut into thin slices.

2. Heat oil in skillet, add bell pepper, coppa, onion, chili pepper and garlic, cook, stirring, 2 minutes. Add spinach, cook, stirring, further 2 minutes.

3. Stir in cheese and pepper. Serve tossed through hot spiral pasta.

Serves 4.

Note: Recipe best made just before serving. Not suitable to freeze.

PUTTANESCA

YOU WILL NEED
**4 ripe tomatoes
12 pimiento stuffed olives
2oz can anchovies
2 cloves garlic
¼ cup olive oil
4 teaspoons chopped
  fresh basil
⅛ teaspoon chili powder
½ cup chopped fresh
  parsley**

Note: Recipe best made just before serving. Not suitable to freeze. Drained canned tomatoes can be used in place of fresh tomatoes, if preferred.

1. Peel and chop tomatoes; slice olives. Drain and chop anchovies; mince garlic.

2. Heat oil in skillet, add garlic, cook, stirring, until garlic just changes color. Add tomatoes, olives, anchovies, basil, chili powder and parsley, cook, stirring, 3 minutes.

Serves 4.

BOLOGNESE

Salsa alla Bolognese (ragù)

YOU WILL NEED
**3 tablespoons olive oil
1 large onion, finely chopped
1½lb ground beef
14½oz can tomatoes
⅓ cup tomato paste
1 teaspoon dried basil leaves
1 teaspoon dried oregano
   leaves
½ teaspoon dried thyme
   leaves
4 cups water
⅛ teaspoon ground black
   pepper
grated fresh Parmesan
   cheese**

1. Heat oil in skillet, add onion, cook, stirring, until lightly browned. Add beef, cook, stirring, until well browned, mashing to break any lumps. Drain away excess fat.

2. Sieve undrained tomatoes into skillet; discard seeds. Add paste, herbs, water and pepper; mix well.

3. Simmer very gently, uncovered, about 1¾ hours or until nearly all the liquid has evaporated. Serve topped with Parmesan cheese.

Serves 4 to 6.

Note: *Recipe can be made 3 days ahead. Reheat just before serving. Suitable to freeze. A traditional bolognese sauce does not contain garlic, however, 2 minced cloves of garlic can be added with the onion in Step 1, if desired.*

CHILI

Peperoncino Piccante

YOU WILL NEED
**4 green onions
3 fresh red chili peppers
2 cloves garlic
½lb dried spaghetti
½ cup (1 stick) butter
3 tablespoons chopped
   fresh parsley**

1. Finely chop green onions. Seed chili peppers, chop finely. Mince garlic.

2. Add spaghetti to large pan of boiling water, boil, uncovered, until just tender; drain well. Heat butter in skillet, add onions, chili peppers and garlic, cook, stirring, 2 minutes. Add spaghetti and parsley, stir to combine. Serve topped with grated Parmesan cheese, if desired.

Serves 2.

Note: *Recipe best made just before serving. Not suitable to freeze. A tablespoon of bottled, chopped chilies can be used in place of fresh chilies, if preferred.*

SPINACH LASAGNE

Lasagne Verdi

YOU WILL NEED
2 teaspoons olive oil
6 sheets lasagne pasta
2 teaspoons olive oil, extra
10oz package frozen spinach
**½ cup grated cheddar
cheese**
**¼ cup grated fresh
Parmesan cheese**

MEAT SAUCE
1lb ground beef
1 onion, finely chopped
1 clove garlic, minced
**¼lb mushrooms,
finely sliced**
28oz can tomatoes
**½ teaspoon dried oregano
leaves**
1 teaspoon sugar

CHEESE SAUCE
¼ cup (½ stick) butter
⅓ cup all-purpose flour
⅛ teaspoon ground nutmeg
2 cups milk
1 cup grated cheddar cheese
**¼ cup grated fresh
Parmesan cheese**

1. Fill large pan two-thirds full with water, add oil, bring to boil. Add pasta sheets separately to pan, allowing water to return to boil before adding the next sheet. If pan is large enough, 3 sheets can be cooked at one time. It is important to add the pasta gradually and cook up to 3 sheets at one time; the oil will help prevent water boiling over and prevent pasta sticking together. Boil, uncovered, about 25 minutes or until very tender. Have ready a large bowl of cold water to which the extra oil has been added. Carefully lift pasta sheets from pan, place into cold water. Replenish the pan with more boiling water, if necessary. Cook remaining pasta in the same way.

2. Place 2 pasta sheets over base of shallow 7 inch x 11 inch ovenproof dish; trimming to fit dish if necessary.

3. Spread half the meat sauce over pasta, cover with half the cheese sauce.

4. Press as much liquid as possible from spinach, spread evenly over cheese sauce. Top with 2 more pasta sheets, spread with remaining meat sauce and cheese sauce, top with remaining pasta sheets.

5. Sprinkle with combined cheeses, bake in 350°F oven about 40 minutes or until lightly browned. Stand 10 minutes before serving.

Meat Sauce: Cook beef in pan, stirring, until well browned; drain away any excess fat. Add onion, garlic and mushrooms, cook, stirring, until onion is soft. Sieve undrained tomatoes into pan; discard seeds. Stir in oregano and sugar, simmer, covered, 45 minutes. Simmer, uncovered, about 15 minutes or until sauce is thick.

Cheese Sauce: Melt butter in pan, add flour and nutmeg, cook, stirring, 1 minute. Remove from heat, gradually add milk, stir over heat until sauce boils and thickens, simmer 1 minute. Remove from heat, stir in cheeses, stir until smooth.
Serves 6.

Note: *Lasagne can be prepared a day ahead. Sauces can be made 2 days ahead. Bake just before serving. Uncooked lasagne suitable to freeze. Meat sauce and cheese sauce are easier to spread if made a day ahead.*

RAVIOLI

YOU WILL NEED
1 egg yolk
4 teaspoons water, extra

PASTA
4 cups all-purpose flour
2 eggs
4 teaspoons olive oil
1 cup water, approximately

FILLING
½lb ground beef
½lb chopped cooked chicken
2oz salami, chopped
2 slices bacon, chopped
¼lb cooked ham, chopped
4 cloves garlic, minced
½ cup chopped fresh parsley
½ teaspoon all-spice
½ cup chopped cooked spinach, drained
2 eggs, lightly beaten

SAUCE
3oz (¾ stick) butter
4 teaspoons olive oil
2 cloves garlic, minced
28oz can tomatoes
½ teaspoon all-spice
½ teaspoon dried rosemary leaves
½ teaspoon dried basil leaves

2. Gradually add ravioli to large pan of boiling water, boil, uncovered, 20 minutes; drain well. Bring sauce to boil in pan, add ravioli, simmer very gently, uncovered, 10 minutes.

Pasta: Sift flour into bowl, add combined eggs and oil. Stir in enough of the water to mix to a firm but pliable dough. Do not have dough too soft or it will be difficult to handle. Turn dough onto lightly floured surface, knead 5 minutes. Place dough into lightly oiled bowl, cover, stand 30 minutes before rolling.

Filling: Process all ingredients together until finely chopped and well combined.

Sauce: Heat butter and oil in pan, add garlic, cook, stirring, 1 minute. Sieve undrained tomatoes into pan; discard seeds. Stir in remaining ingredients, simmer gently, covered, 1 hour, stirring sauce occasionally.

Serves 6.

1. Roll out half the pasta until ¹⁄₁₆ inch thick. Cut into 4 inch wide strips. Place teaspoons of filling at 2 inch intervals along one edge of pasta strips. Brush edge of pasta with combined egg yolk and water, fold in half, press edges firmly; cut into ravioli shapes using pastry cutter. Repeat with remaining pasta, filling and egg yolk mixture.

Note: Ravioli and sauce can be made 2 days ahead. Cook ravioli just before serving. Sauce and uncooked ravioli suitable to freeze. Pasta dough can be made in a food processor and rolled using a pasta machine, if preferred.

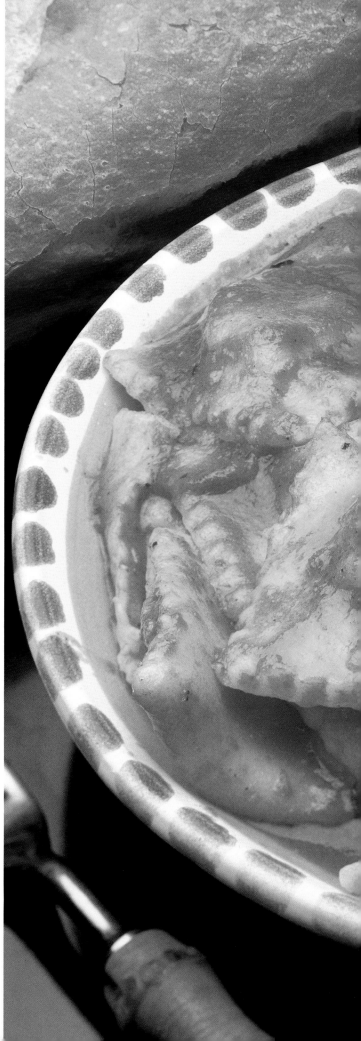

SUPPLI

YOU WILL NEED
1 tablespoon butter
1 small onion, chopped
1½ cups long-grain rice
½ cup dry white wine
2½ cups hot water
⅛ teaspoon ground saffron
1 teaspoon chicken instant bouillon
1 tablespoon butter, extra
4 teaspoons grated fresh Parmesan cheese
2 eggs, lightly beaten
3oz mozzarella cheese
⅔ cup packaged unseasoned bread crumbs
oil for deep-frying

The full name of these delicious little rice balls is Suppli al Telefono – meaning "croquettes on the telephone". The name comes about because when pulled apart after cooking, the hot cheese in the center runs into strings like telephone wires.

1. Heat butter in pan, add onion, cook, stirring, until soft. Add rice, cook, stirring, 2 minutes. Add wine, half the water, saffron and instant bouillon. Boil, uncovered, until water has almost been absorbed. Add remaining water, simmer, uncovered, about 12 minutes or until all water has been absorbed. Stir in extra butter and Parmesan cheese; cool.

Add eggs, stir gently, taking care not to mash the rice. Cut mozzarella into ½ inch cubes.

2. Place a tablespoon of rice in one hand, add a cube of cheese, then cover cheese with another tablespoon of rice. Shape into a ball, completely enclosing cheese. Roll balls in bread crumbs. Balls can be fried at once but are easier to handle if refrigerated a few hours.

3. Deep-fry balls in batches in hot oil until they are golden brown; drain on absorbent paper. Serve while hot.
Makes about 18.

Note: Recipe can be prepared a day ahead. Deep-fry balls just before serving. Not suitable to freeze.

RISOTTO MILANESE

YOU WILL NEED
¼ cup (½ stick) butter
1 large onion, finely chopped
¾lb long-grain rice
½ cup dry white wine
3 cups hot water
¼ teaspoon ground saffron
2 chicken bouillon cubes
2 tablespoons (¼ stick) butter, extra
3 tablespoons grated fresh Parmesan cheese

1. Heat butter in skillet, add onion, cook, stirring, until soft.

2. Add rice, stir until well coated with butter mixture. Add wine, 1 cup of the water, saffron and crumbled bouillon cubes. Boil, uncovered, until almost all the water has been absorbed, stirring occasionally. Add half the remaining hot water, stir well, boil, uncovered, until water has almost been absorbed, stirring occasionally. Stir in remaining hot water, simmer, uncovered, until water has been absorbed, stirring occasionally. Total cooking time for risotto is about 20 minutes.

3. Stir in extra butter and cheese, stir gently until butter is just melted.
Serves 6.

Note: Recipe best made just before serving. Not suitable to freeze.

GNOCCHI & POLENTA

Gnocchi can be served as an appetizer or part of a main course. Polenta, from northern Italy, is a traditional meal accompaniment.

SPINACH GNOCCHI

Gnocchi di Spinaci

YOU WILL NEED
1¼lb spinach or
    Swiss chard
½lb ricotta cheese
1 cup grated fresh
    Parmesan cheese
1 egg, lightly beaten
¼ teaspoon ground nutmeg
all-purpose flour
3 tablespoons butter, melted

2. Mold a rounded tablespoon of mixture into a ball or egg shape using a spoon and palm of hand; place onto tray covered with sifted flour. Repeat with remaining mixture.

4. Simmer gently about 2 minutes or until gnocchi rise to surface. Remove from pan with slotted spoon.

1. Wash and dry spinach, remove white stalks. Cook spinach leaves, without boiling, in large pan with a tight-fitting lid until just tender. Drain well, chop finely. Combine spinach, ricotta cheese, half the Parmesan cheese, egg and nutmeg in bowl; mix well.

3. Roll gnocchi in flour. Gradually add gnocchi to large pan of boiling water.

5. Arrange gnocchi in well greased ovenproof dish in single layer. Pour over butter, sprinkle with remaining Parmesan cheese. Cook under hot broiler until cheese is lightly browned.

Serves 4 to 6 as an appetizer.

Note: *Recipe can be prepared 3 hours ahead. Mold and cook gnocchi just before serving. Not suitable to freeze.*

GNOCCHI ALLA ROMANA

YOU WILL NEED
3 cups milk
¼ teaspoon salt
⅛ teaspoon ground nutmeg
⅔ cup semolina
1 egg, lightly beaten
1½ cups grated Parmesan cheese
¼ cup (½ stick) butter, melted

1. Bring milk, salt and nutmeg to boil in pan. Reduce heat, gradually add semolina.

2. Boil, stirring, about 10 minutes or until very thick. A wooden spoon should stand upright in center of pan when mixture is ready. Remove from heat. Stir in combined egg and 1 cup of the cheese; mix well.

3. Spread mixture into oiled jelly-roll pan, smoothing with wet spatula until ¼ inch thick. Cover, refrigerate about 1 hour or until firm.

4. Turn firm semolina onto board, cut into 1½ inch rounds using a cutter. Arrange rounds in overlapping circles in shallow greased ovenproof dish, pour over butter, sprinkle with remaining cheese. Bake in 350°F oven about 15 minutes or until crisp and lightly browned. Serves 4 to 6.

Note: Recipe can be prepared a day ahead. Bake just before serving. Not suitable to freeze.

POLENTA

YOU WILL NEED
8 cups water
¼ teaspoon salt
2 cups yellow cornmeal
¼ cup olive oil

This is a speciality of northern Italy, particularly popular around Venice. Served plain, it is generally accompanied by a ragout such as bolognese sauce; or, firm it can be fried and served as an accompaniment to any meat. Hot, fried polenta also can be topped with anchovies and olives or other toppings and served as crostini.

1. Bring water and salt to boil in large pan. Gradually sprinkle cornmeal over water, stirring constantly to prevent lumps forming. Reduce heat to low (this is important, as mixture may bubble and spatter; partially covering the pan is a good idea). Simmer about 30 minutes or until polenta is very thick, stirring often. A wooden spoon should stand upright in center of pan when mixture is ready. The polenta can be served at this point, piled onto a plate or fried as shown in the following steps.

2. Spread mixture evenly into an oiled shallow 7 inch x 11 inch baking pan. Cool, stand at room temperature about 3 hours or until firm.

3. Turn polenta onto board. Cut into 1½ inch slices or into squares. Heat oil in skillet until very hot, add polenta slices, cook gently about 5 minutes, or until polenta is golden brown on both sides. Serves 4 to 6.

Note: Recipe can be prepared a day ahead. Cut and fry just before serving. Not suitable to freeze. Chicken or vegetable instant bouillon can be added to the water for extra flavor, if desired.

PIZZA

YOU WILL NEED
- 1 package (¼oz) active dry yeast
- ½ teaspoon sugar
- ½ cup lukewarm water
- 1½ cups all-purpose flour
- 3 tablespoons olive oil
- 1¼ cups shredded mozzarella cheese
- 3 tablespoons grated Parmesan cheese
- 2oz can anchovies, drained
- 1 small red bell pepper, chopped
- 3 button mushrooms, finely sliced
- 5 black olives

FILLING
- 2 teaspoons olive oil
- 1 onion, finely chopped
- 1 clove garlic, minced
- 14½oz can tomatoes
- 4 teaspoons tomato paste
- ½ teaspoon dried oregano leaves
- ½ teaspoon dried basil leaves
- 1 teaspoon sugar

1. Combine yeast, sugar and lukewarm water in bowl, stand 10 minutes or until frothy. Sift flour into bowl, make well in center, add oil and yeast mixture. Mix to a firm dough by hand.

2. Turn dough onto floured surface, knead about 10 minutes or until dough is smooth and elastic. Place in lightly oiled bowl, cover, stand in warm place about 30 minutes or until doubled in size; knock down.

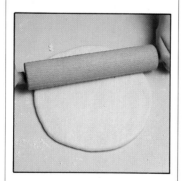

3. Knead dough into smooth ball. Flatten into a circle about 1 inch thick. Roll from center to edge until large enough to fit 10 inch pizza pan.

4. Spread filling evenly over pizza base.

5. Sprinkle half combined cheeses over pizza. Top with anchovies, pepper and mushrooms. Sprinkle with olives then remaining cheese. Bake in 400°F oven about 20 minutes or until crust is cooked underneath and golden brown.

Filling: Heat oil in pan, add onion and garlic, cook, stirring, until onion is soft. Add undrained crushed tomatoes and remaining ingredients, simmer, uncovered, stirring occasionally, about 10 minutes or until mixture is thick; cool.

Serves 4 to 6.

Note: *Recipe can be prepared 1 hour ahead; keep in refrigerator. Bake just before serving. Filling can be made 2 days ahead. Filling and uncooked pizza suitable to freeze. Bake straight from freezer, allowing an extra 10 minutes cooking time.*

FISH & SHELLFISH

Perhaps it is with fish and shellfish that Italian cooking is at its most subtle, flavorful best.

FRIED SARDINES — *Sarde Fritte*

YOU WILL NEED
12 sardines
all-purpose flour
1 egg, lightly beaten
3 tablespoons milk
2 cups fresh bread crumbs
1 cup light olive oil
lemon wedges

HERBED BUTTER
½ cup (1 stick) butter
2 teaspoons chopped
    fresh parsley
1 green onion,
    finely chopped
1 clove garlic, minced

2. Open sardines out flat. Cut through backbones at tail end, as shown. Gently lever out backbones, starting from tail end. Wash sardines; pat dry.

4. Heat oil and reserved herbed butter in skillet, add sardines, cook until golden brown on both sides and cooked through; drain on absorbent paper. Serve with herbed butter and lemon .

Herbed Butter: Beat butter in small bowl until smooth and creamy. Add parsley, onion and garlic; beat well. Spoon half the butter into small bowl, cover, refrigerate until firm. Reserve remaining herbed butter for frying sardines.

Serves 4 as an appetizer.

1. Scale sardines with back of knife, working from tail toward head; cut away head. Using scissors, cut underside open, remove entrails.

3. Coat sardines lightly in flour, dip in combined egg and milk, then in bread crumbs to coat.

Note: Sardines can be crumbed a day ahead. Cook just before serving. Herbed butter can be made 2 days ahead. Uncooked crumbed sardines and herbed butter suitable to freeze.

FISH WITH ZUCCHINI

Pesce con Zucchini

YOU WILL NEED
4 small fish fillets
¾lb small zucchini
6 leaves fresh basil
14½oz can tomatoes
¼ cup (½ stick) butter
3 tablespoons olive oil
1in sprig fresh rosemary
**4 teaspoons packaged
   unseasoned bread crumbs**
**2 teaspoons fresh
   lemon juice**
1 tablespoon butter, extra

1. Remove skin from fish, remove bones. Slice zucchini, finely chop basil. Sieve undrained tomatoes into bowl; discard seeds.

2. Melt butter in large skillet, add fish. Cook gently until golden brown on both sides, turning once. Arrange fish in single layer in base of greased ovenproof dish.

3. Heat oil in skillet, add zucchini, cook, stirring, until lightly browned. Add rosemary, half the basil and tomatoes. Simmer, uncovered, 3 minutes, remove and discard rosemary.

4. Spoon tomato mixture over fish in dish. Sprinkle over combined bread crumbs and remaining basil, drizzle with juice, dot with extra butter. Bake, uncovered, in 375°F oven about 10 minutes or until browned. Serves 2.

Note: *Recipe best made just before serving. Not suitable to freeze.*

FISH MILANESE

Pesce alla Milanese

YOU WILL NEED
4 fish fillets
**1 small onion,
   finely chopped**
**3 tablespoons fresh lemon
   juice**
⅓ cup light olive oil
all-purpose flour
2 eggs, lightly beaten
**4 teaspoons milk
packaged unseasoned
   bread crumbs**
**4 teaspoons light olive oil,
   extra**
¼ cup (½ stick) butter
¼ cup (½ stick) butter, extra
1 clove garlic, minced
**2 teaspoons chopped
   fresh parsley**

1. Remove skin from fish, remove bones. Combine onion, juice and oil in large dish; mix well. Add fish, spoon oil mixture over fish to coat thoroughly, cover, refrigerate 1 hour, turning occasionally.

2. Remove fish from marinade, coat lightly in flour, dip in combined eggs and milk, then into bread crumbs, pressing crumbs on firmly.

3. Heat extra oil and butter in large skillet. Add fish, cook until golden brown on both sides, turning once; drain on absorbent paper. Melt extra butter in separate skillet, add garlic, cook, stirring, until butter is light golden brown; add parsley. Pour browned butter over fish. Serves 4.

Note: *Fish can be crumbed a day ahead. Cook just before serving. Not suitable to freeze.*

FRITTO MISTO

YOU WILL NEED
1lb uncooked jumbo shrimp
1lb small cleaned squid
½lb fish fillets
½lb sea scallops
oil for deep-frying
BATTER
1 cup self-rising flour
¼ teaspoon baking soda
1 cup water, approximately

1. Shell and devein shrimp, leaving tails intact. Cut squid into thin rings. Remove bones from fish, cut fish into bite-sized pieces. Clean scallops.
  Dip shrimp, squid, fish and scallops into batter; drain away excess batter.

2. Deep-fry in batches in hot oil until golden brown and cooked; drain on absorbent paper. Serve hot with tartare sauce.

Batter: Sift flour and soda into bowl, gradually add water, beat to a smooth batter. Add a little extra water if batter is too thick. Serves 6 as an appetizer.

Note: Batter can be made 2 hours ahead. Cook seafood just before serving. Not suitable to freeze. Do not have the oil too hot to prevent overbrowning.

TARTARE SAUCE

Salsa Tartara

YOU WILL NEED
2 egg yolks
¼ teaspoon salt
1 teaspoon white vinegar
1 cup light olive oil
2 tablespoons fresh lemon juice
2 green onions
2 teaspoons capers
1 dill pickle
4 sprigs fresh parsley

Blender Method: Blend or process egg yolks, salt and vinegar until smooth. While motor is operating, add oil gradually in a thin stream. When all oil has been added, add juice and 4 teaspoons of water.

Hand Method: Pour hot water into a bowl, pour water out, dry bowl thoroughly. Combine egg yolks, salt and vinegar in bowl. Whisk vigorously with wire whisk, add oil gradually, whisking between additions. When all oil has been added, add juice. (As hand beaten mayonnaise is slightly thinner than blender method, water is not needed.)

Finely chop green onions, capers, dill pickle and parsley; stir into mayonnaise.

Note: Recipe can be made 1 week ahead. Cover suface of sauce with a little oil; store in refrigerator. Not suitable to freeze.

MARINATED SQUID

YOU WILL NEED
1lb small squid
⅓ cup fresh lemon juice
⅓ cup light olive oil
1 clove garlic, minced
4 teaspoons chopped
   fresh parsley

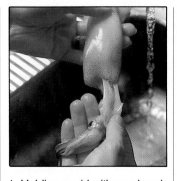

1. Holding squid with one hand, gently pull head and entrails away in one piece. Cut tentacles from head. Remove bone found at open end of squid (it looks like a long, thin piece of plastic).

2. Clean squid under cold running water, then peel away brown outer skin.

3. Cut squid evenly into ¼ inch rings. Drop rings into boiling water, simmer about 15 minutes or until tender; drain. Combine squid and remaining ingredients in bowl, cover, refrigerate overnight. Serve with marinade.

Note: Recipe best made a day ahead. Not suitable to freeze.

FRIED SQUID

YOU WILL NEED
2lb small squid
1 egg, lightly beaten
3 tablespoons milk
packaged unseasoned
   bread crumbs
oil for deep-frying or
   shallow-frying

1. Clean squid as in Steps 1 and 2 above. Cut squid into ¼ inch rings. Dip squid into combined egg and milk, drain away excess. Toss squid in bread crumbs, patting bread crumbs on firmly to coat.

2. Deep-fry squid in batches in hot oil until golden brown; drain on absorbent paper.

3. Alternatively, shallow-fry squid in batches in hot oil until golden brown, turning squid with forks once during cooking; drain on absorbent paper. Serve hot with lemon wedges.
Serves 4.

Note: Squid can be crumbed a day ahead. Cook just before serving. Not suitable to freeze.

MEAT & POULTRY

Veal is a favorite – tender, light, teamed with the richness of melting cheese or colorful sauces. We've added other popular dishes, too.

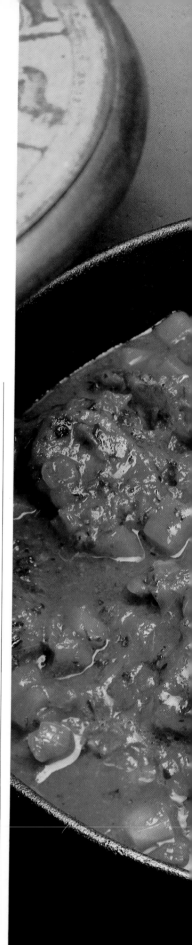

OSSO BUCO

YOU WILL NEED
3oz (¾ stick) butter
2 carrots, chopped
2 large onions,
    finely chopped
3 stalks celery,
    finely chopped
1 clove garlic, minced
4 x 1½lb veal shanks, cut
    into 2½in slices
all-purpose flour
3 tablespoons olive oil
½ cup dry red wine
15oz can beef consomme
1 teaspoon dried basil leaves
1 teaspoon dried thyme
    leaves
1 bay leaf
1in strip lemon peel
28oz can tomatoes

GREMOLADA
1 clove garlic, minced
¼ cup chopped fresh
    parsley
1 teaspoon grated lemon
    zest

Osso Bucco means "hollow bones"; it is served throughout Italy but is a specialty of Milan. The traditional accompaniment is Risotto Milanese, page 48.

1. Heat one-third of the butter in pan. Add carrots, onions, celery and half the garlic. Cook, stirring, until onions are golden brown. Remove from heat. Transfer vegetables to a large ovenproof dish.

2. Toss shanks in flour. Heat remaining butter and oil in large skillet, add shanks, cook until well browned all over.

3. Drain fat from skillet. Add wine, consomme, basil, thyme, bay leaf and lemon peel to skillet. Sieve undrained tomatoes into skillet; discard seeds. Stir over heat until boiling.

4. Carefully pack shanks upright on top of vegetables in dish. Pour sauce over shanks, bake, covered, in 350°F oven about 1½ hours or until veal is very tender, stirring occasionally. Serve osso buco sprinkled with gremolada.
Gremolada: Combine garlic, parsley and zest in bowl.
Serves 6.

Note: Recipe can be made a day ahead. Reheat just before serving. Suitable to freeze.

VEAL CAMPAGNOLA
Vitello alla Campagnola

YOU WILL NEED
**5 Swiss chard leaves,
shredded**
**2 tablespoons (¼ stick)
butter**
4 veal steaks
all-purpose flour
**2 tablespoons (¼ stick)
butter, extra**
1 tablespoon olive oil
**4 slices mozzarella or
gruyere cheese**

TOMATO SAUCE
**2 tablespoons (¼ stick)
butter**
2 cloves garlic, minced
14½oz can tomatoes
4 teaspoons tomato paste
¼ cup dry white wine
¼ cup water
1 teaspoon sugar

1. Place Swiss chard in pan with enough water to cover bottom of pan. Simmer, covered, until tender; drain well. Toss with butter. Trim veal, pound gently with meat mallet until thin. Toss steaks in flour, shake away excess flour.

2. Heat extra butter and oil in skillet, add veal, cook, turning once, until almost cooked through; remove skillet from heat. Divide Swiss chard over veal, top with cheese.

3. Pour tomato sauce around veal, taking care not to cover the cheese, cover, simmer gently about 10 minutes or until cheese is melted.
Tomato Sauce: Heat butter in pan, add garlic, cook 1 minute. Sieve undrained tomatoes into pan; discard seeds. Stir in paste, wine, water and sugar, simmer, uncovered, 5 minutes. Serves 4.

Note: Sauce can be made 2 days ahead. Recipe best made just before serving. Sauce suitable to freeze.

TRIPE VENETIAN-STYLE
Trippa alla Veneziana

YOU WILL NEED
2lb tripe
3 tablespoons olive oil
**2 tablespoons (¼ stick)
butter**
1 onion, chopped
1 carrot, chopped
2 stalks celery, chopped
2 cloves garlic, minced
**3 tablespoons chopped
fresh parsley**
1 teaspoon dried basil leaves
**½ teaspoon dried oregano
leaves**
14½oz can tomatoes
4 teaspoons tomato paste
1 teaspoon sugar
½ cup dry red wine
½ cup water
1 beef bouillon cube
**¼ cup grated fresh
Parmesan cheese**

1. Rinse tripe under cold water. Cut into 1 inch x 3 inch strips. Place tripe in pan, cover with cold water, bring to boil; drain.

2. Heat oil and butter in skillet, add onion, carrot and celery, cook, stirring, until onion is soft. Add garlic, parsley, basil and oregano, cook, stirring, 2 minutes. Sieve undrained tomatoes into bowl; discard seeds. Add tripe, tomatoes, paste and sugar to skillet, simmer, uncovered, 5 minutes.

3. Add wine, water and crumbled bouillon cube, bring to boil, pour into ovenproof dish. Cover, bake in 325°F oven 2 hours. Remove from oven; stir in cheese just before serving. Serves 4.

Note: Recipe can be made several hours ahead. Reheat just before serving. Not suitable to freeze.

VITELLO TONNATO

YOU WILL NEED
3lb boneless veal loin roast
2oz can anchovies, drained
1 clove garlic
2 carrots, chopped
3 stalks celery, chopped
2 onions, quartered
6 sprigs parsley
5 cups water
2 chicken bouillon cubes
1½ cups dry white wine

TUNA SAUCE
2 tablespoons capers
¾ cup light olive oil
1 egg yolk
3½oz can tuna, drained
3 tablespoons fresh
**   lemon juice**
¼ cup heavy cream

1. Using tip of sharp knife, make small cuts along length of veal. Cut 4 anchovies into ½ inch lengths; reserve remaining anchovies for sauce. Cut garlic into slivers. Insert anchovy and garlic pieces into each cut. Place veal in pan, cover with cold water, bring to boil, boil, uncovered, 1 minute. Drain veal, rinse under water.

2. Place veal in pan, with carrots, celery, onions, parsley, water, crumbled bouillon cubes and wine. Simmer, partly covered, about 1½ to 2 hours or until veal is tender. Remove veal from broth; cool. Reserve ¼ cup broth for tuna sauce.

3. Cut veal into thin slices, arrange on serving plate, spoon over some of the sauce. Garnish with salad greens, black olives and sieved cooked egg yolk, if desired. Serve with remaining tuna sauce .

Tuna Sauce: Cover reserved anchovies with water, stand 10 minutes; drain, pat dry. Wash capers under cold water, drain; chop finely. Blend or process anchovies, oil, egg yolk, tuna and juice until smooth. Transfer mixture to bowl, stir in cream, reserved veal broth and capers. Serves 6.

Note: *Recipe can be prepared a day ahead. Serve cold. Not suitable to freeze.*

VEAL PARMESAN

Vitello al Parmigiano

YOU WILL NEED
4 pieces veal steak
all-purpose flour
1 egg, lightly beaten
4 teaspoons water
packaged unseasoned
**   bread crumbs**
2 tablespoons (¼ stick)
**   butter**
¼ cup olive oil
½lb shredded mozzarella
**   cheese**
¼ cup grated fresh
**   Parmesan cheese**
4 teaspoons olive oil, extra

TOMATO SAUCE
4 teaspoons olive oil
1 onion, finely chopped
1 stalk celery, finely chopped
1 red bell pepper,
**   finely chopped**
1 clove garlic, minced
14½oz can tomatoes
4 teaspoons chopped
**   fresh parsley**
½ teaspoon dried basil
**   leaves**
2 teaspoons sugar
4 teaspoons tomato paste
1½ cups water
1 chicken bouillon cube

1. Pound veal gently using a meat mallet until thin, trim, remove membrane from edge of veal. Toss veal in flour, shake away excess flour. Dip veal in combined egg and water, then in bread crumbs to coat, refrigerate while preparing tomato sauce.

Heat butter and oil in skillet, add veal, cook until browned and almost cooked. Place veal in ovenproof dish, sprinkle with mozzarella cheese.

2. Spoon tomato sauce over mozzarella cheese.

3. Sprinkle evenly with Parmesan cheese, drizzle with extra oil. Bake, uncovered, in 350°F oven 20 minutes.
Tomato Sauce: Heat oil in pan, add onion, celery, pepper and garlic, cook, stirring, until onion is soft. Sieve undrained tomatoes into pan. Stir in remaining ingredients. Simmer, uncovered, about 20 minutes or until thick.
Serves 4.

Note: *Recipe can be prepared 6 hours ahead. Bake just before serving. Sauce suitable to freeze.*

VEAL MARSALA

YOU WILL NEED
4 veal steaks
ground black pepper
all-purpose flour
2 tablespoons (¼ stick)
    butter
3 tablespoons olive oil
⅓ cup marsala
1 chicken bouillon cube
½ cup water

1. Season veal with pepper on both sides. Toss veal in flour, shake away excess flour.

2. Heat butter and oil in skillet, add veal, cook 2 minutes each side; drain on absorbent paper. Drain away butter and oil from skillet. Add marsala, crumbled bouillon cube and half the water to skillet, boil, stirring, 2 minutes.

3. Return veal to skillet, simmer gently, covered, 5 minutes, turning veal once. Place veal on serving plate; keep warm. Add remaining water to skillet, simmer, stirring, until sauce is a syrupy glaze, spoon over veal. Serves 4.

Note: *Recipe best made just before serving. Not suitable to freeze.*

CHICKEN MARSALA

YOU WILL NEED
¼ cup (½ stick) butter
1 clove garlic, minced
4 boneless, skinless chicken
    breast halves
4 slices mozzarella cheese
12 capers
4 canned anchovies, drained
4 teaspoons chopped fresh
    parsley
¼ cup marsala
⅔ cup heavy cream

1. Melt butter in skillet, add garlic and chicken, cook until chicken is lightly browned all over; remove from skillet. Arrange a slice of cheese, 3 capers and 1 anchovy over each chicken breast, sprinkle with parsley.

2. Carefully return chicken to skillet, cook, covered, about 5 minutes or until just cooked through. Remove from skillet; keep warm.

3. Add marsala and cream to skillet, simmer gently, stirring, until sauce is slightly thickened. Spoon sauce over chicken just before serving. Serves 4.

Note: *Recipe best made just before serving. Not suitable to freeze.*

CHICKEN CACCIATORE

Pollo alla Cacciatora

YOU WILL NEED

3lb chicken (or chicken pieces)
3 tablespoons olive oil
1 onion, finely chopped
1 clove garlic
½ cup dry white wine
2 tablespoons vinegar
1 chicken bouillon cube
½ cup water
14½oz can tomatoes
1 teaspoon dried basil leaves
1 teaspoon sugar
3 canned anchovies, drained
¼ cup milk
¼ cup black olives, pitted, halved
4 teaspoons chopped fresh parsley

1. Cut chicken into serving-sized pieces. Heat oil in skillet, add chicken, cook until browned all over. Place chicken in ovenproof dish.

2. Drain away all but 1 tablespoon pan juices from skillet. Add onion and garlic, cook, stirring, until onion is soft. Add wine and vinegar, boil, uncovered, until reduced by half. Add crumbled bouillon cube and water, stir over high heat 2 minutes. Sieve undrained tomatoes into bowl; discard seeds. Add tomatoes, basil and sugar to skillet, simmer, uncovered, 1 minute.

3. Pour tomato mixture over chicken, bake, covered, in 350°F oven 1 hour.

Combine anchovies and milk in bowl, stand 5 minutes, drain; chop finely. Arrange chicken in serving dish; keep warm. Pour liquid from ovenproof dish into pan, boil, uncovered, 1 minute. Add anchovies, olives and parsley, simmer 2 minutes; pour over chicken.

Serves 4.

Note: *Recipe can be made a day ahead. Reheat just before serving.*

VEAL CASSEROLE

Vitello in Umido

YOU WILL NEED

8 veal chops
¼ cup (½ stick) butter
2 onions, quartered
3 cloves garlic, minced
1 bulb fennel, sliced
¼lb pancetta, chopped
2oz button mushrooms, sliced
¾ cup dry white wine
1 cup water
1 chicken bouillon cube
4 teaspoons tomato paste
3 tablespoons all-purpose flour
3 tablespoons water, extra

1. Remove any fat and gristle from chops.

2. Melt butter in skillet, add chops, cook until well browned on both sides. Place chops in ovenproof dish in single layer.

3. Add onions, garlic, fennel, pancetta and mushrooms to skillet, cook, stirring, 2 minutes. Add wine, water, crumbled bouillon cube and paste, bring to boil.

4. Pour vegetable mixture over chops, bake, covered, in 350°F oven about 45 minutes or until chops are tender. Remove chops from dish; keep warm. Pour sauce and vegetables into pan, stir in blended flour and extra water. Stir over heat until mixture boils and thickens, pour over chops.

Serves 4.

Note: *Recipe can be made a day ahead. Reheat just before serving. Not suitable to freeze. Pancetta is a specially cured bacon, available from most delicatessens. If unavailable, substitute ham.*

STUFFED VEAL SCALLOPS

Scaloppine di Vitello Ripiene

YOU WILL NEED
8 veal steaks
2 tablespoons (¼ stick)
butter
5oz button mushrooms,
sliced
4 thin slices cooked ham
⅓ cup grated fresh
Parmesan cheese
¼ cup (½ stick) butter, extra
4 slices mozzarella cheese
½ cup hot water
½ beef bouillon cube

1. Gently pound veal with meat mallet until thin. Melt butter in skillet, add mushrooms, cook, stirring, until mushrooms are just soft; drain.

2. Top 4 veal steaks with ham, mushrooms then Parmesan cheese. Place remaining veal steaks on top, trimming edges if necessary.

3. Melt extra butter in skillet, add veal, cook until browned underneath, carefully turn veal, brown on other side, remove skillet from heat. Cover veal with mozzarella cheese, trimming if necessary. Add combined water and crumbled bouillon cube to skillet, simmer, covered, about 2 minutes or until mozzarella cheese is melted.

Serves 4.

Note: *Recipe best made just before serving. Not suitable to freeze.*

DUCK WITH ANCHOVY SAUCE

Anitra alle Acciughe

YOU WILL NEED
3lb duck
2 tablespoons (¼ stick)
butter, melted
4 slices bacon, chopped
1 onion, chopped
3 cloves garlic, minced
½ teaspoon dried rosemary
leaves
½ teaspoon dried sage
leaves
3 tablespoons fresh
lemon juice
2oz can anchovies,
finely chopped
1 cup dry red wine
1½ cups water
4 teaspoons red wine
vinegar
3 tablespoons all-purpose
flour
½ cup water, extra
¼ cup heavy cream

1. Wash duck under cold water; pat dry, retain neck. Tie legs together with string, tuck wings under body. Place duck breast-side-up on wire rack in roasting pan, brush with butter. Bake in 350°F oven 20 minutes. Remove from oven, prick skin all over with fork, turn breast-side-down, brush with butter. Bake further 20 minutes. Turn duck, bake further 50 minutes.

2. Combine bacon, onion, garlic, rosemary, sage and duck neck in pan, cook, stirring, 4 minutes. Add juice and anchovies, cook, stirring, 1 minute. Add wine, water and vinegar to pan, simmer, covered, 20 minutes.

3. Remove and discard duck neck. Strain sauce into bowl, pressing mixture firmly in strainer to extract juices; reserve sauce.

4. Remove duck from oven, cut away string, cut duck into quarters. Pour all but 4 teaspoons of juices from roasting pan. Add flour to pan, cook, stirring, until browned. Remove from heat, gradually add extra water, stir until mixture is smooth. Add reserved sauce, stir over heat until mixture boils and thickens. Stir in cream, pour over duck.

Serves 4.

Note: *Recipe best made just before serving. Not suitable to freeze.*

SALADS AND & VEGETABLES

Crisp, colorful salads provide variety. Here, too, are interesting ways with vegetables; some can be served as an appetizer or a light main course.

SQUID & VEGETABLE SALAD

Calamari con Verdure in Insalata

YOU WILL NEED
2oz can anchovies, drained
3 cloves garlic
1 teaspoon chopped fresh parsley
4 teaspoons olive oil
4 small cleaned squid
1 egg, lightly beaten
1 cup packaged unseasoned bread crumbs
oil for deep-frying
1 small cucumber
3 ripe tomatoes, quartered
2 teaspoons finely chopped fresh basil
1 green bell pepper, thinly sliced
1 avocado, chopped
¼ cup black olives
2 teaspoons dried oregano leaves
3 tablespoons olive oil, extra
4 teaspoons white wine vinegar
ground black pepper
4 large lettuce leaves

1. Place anchovies in small bowl. Add 1 clove minced garlic, parsley and oil, stand while preparing salad.

2. Cut cleaned squid into thin rings. Dip squid into egg, then in bread crumbs to coat. Deep-fry squid in batches in hot oil until golden brown; drain on absorbent paper.

3. Thinly slice cucumber. Combine cucumber, remaining minced garlic, tomatoes, basil, bell pepper, avocado, olives and oregano in bowl. Combine extra oil, vinegar and black pepper in jar; shake well. Add to salad, toss gently.

4. Tear lettuce into pieces, place in serving bowl, top with salad. Arrange squid around edge of salad, arrange anchovies in center of salad spoon over anchovy marinade.

Serves 4 to 6.

Note: *Recipe best made just before serving. Not suitable to freeze.*

VEGETABLE SALAD

Insalata Mista

YOU WILL NEED
2 ripe tomatoes
⅓ cup green olives
⅓ cup black olives
2 Belgian endives
1 red leaf lettuce
1 bunch chicory

DRESSING
¼ cup white vinegar
½ cup olive oil
2 tablespoons chopped
**   fresh basil**
ground black pepper
pinch sugar

1. Cut tomatoes into quarters.

2. Combine tomatoes and olives in bowl, pour over dressing, mix lightly; stand 30 minutes.

3. Separate endive leaves. Arrange endive, lettuce and chicory on large platter. Place tomatoes and olives in center. Spoon dressing over top of salad just before serving.
Dressing: Whisk all ingredients in bowl.
Serves 6.

Note: Recipe can be prepared 6 hours ahead. Not suitable to freeze.

BAGNA CAUDA

YOU WILL NEED
2½ cups heavy cream
2 cloves garlic
2oz can anchovies, drained
¼ cup (½ stick) butter

1. Place cream in pan, bring to boil, simmer, uncovered, about 15 minutes or until cream is thickened, stirring frequently. Finely mince garlic. Finely chop drained anchovies.

2. Melt butter in separate pan over low heat, taking care not to brown butter. Add garlic and anchovies, stir until mixture is well blended and is a paste consistency.

3. Stir in hot cream; mix well. Serve warm.
Serves 6.

Note: Recipe best made just before serving. Not suitable to freeze. Serve with crisp, chopped vegetables.

STUFFED TOMATOES

Pomodori Ripieni

YOU WILL NEED
6 firm ripe tomatoes
5 Swiss chard leaves
4 teaspoons pine nuts
2 teaspoons olive oil
⅓ cup long-grain rice
1 tablespoon olive oil, extra
1 small clove garlic, minced
**¼ teaspoon dried basil
    leaves**
ground black pepper
**⅓ cup grated fresh
    Parmesan cheese**

1. Cut tops from tomatoes, carefully scoop out flesh with a teaspoon. Turn tomatoes upside down on absorbent paper to drain.

2. Tear washed Swiss chard into large pieces, place in pan. Stir over heat until tender, drain well; cool.

3. Combine nuts and oil in pan, cook, stirring, until lightly browned; drain immediately. Add rice to pan of boiling water, boil, uncovered, about 12 minutes or until just tender; drain well.

4. Process Swiss chard and nuts until finely chopped.

5. Transfer mixture to bowl, add extra oil, garlic, basil and pepper; mix well. Stir in rice and cheese. Spoon rice mixture into tomatoes, place in greased ovenproof dish. Bake in 350°F oven about 15 minutes or until heated through.

Serves 6.

Note: Recipe can be prepared a day ahead. Bake just before serving. Not suitable to freeze.

EGGPLANT IN A CARRIAGE

Melanzane in Carrozza

YOU WILL NEED
1 large eggplant
¼lb mozzarella cheese
¼ cup olive oil
ground black pepper
**2 tablespoons chopped
    fresh basil**
oil for deep-frying
BATTER
½ teaspoon active dry yeast
2 cups all-purpose flour
2 cups lukewarm water

1. Cut eggplant into ¼ inch slices. Cut mozzarella into ⅛ inch slices.

2. Heat oil in skillet, cook eggplant slices in batches until browned on each side; drain on absorbent paper. Sprinkle eggplant slices with pepper and basil, top half the slices with cheese. Place remaining slices on top, pressing together firmly.

3. Dip an eggplant "sandwich" into batter, drain away excess batter, then deep-fry in hot oil until lightly browned; drain on absorbent paper. Repeat battering and deep-frying with remaining eggplant "sandwiches".
Batter: Sift yeast and flour into bowl, make well in center, add lukewarm water; mix well, stand 30 minutes.

Makes 6 to 8.

Note: Recipe best made just before serving. Not suitable to freeze.

CAULIFLOWER NEAPOLITAN

Cavolfiore alla Napoletana

YOU WILL NEED
8 stuffed green olives
½ small onion
1 small stalk celery
½ cauliflower
½ cup olive oil
3 tablespoons fresh lemon juice
4 capers
3 tablespoons chopped fresh parsley
ground black pepper

1. If desired, remove centers from olives, cut olives into thin slices. Peel and finely slice onion; chop celery. Cut cauliflower into small florets, add to pan of boiling water, boil 5 minutes; drain. Place into bowl of cold water, stand 30 minutes; drain well.

2. Combine olives, onions, celery, oil, juice, capers, parsley and pepper in large bowl. Add cauliflower; toss well.
Serves 4.

__Note:__ Recipe can be made a day ahead. Not suitable to freeze.

TOMATOES AND SALAMI

Pomodori e Salame

YOU WILL NEED
¼lb sliced salami
⅓ cup olive oil
4 teaspoons fresh lemon juice
½ teaspoon grated lemon zest
ground black pepper
1 clove garlic, minced
4 teaspoons chopped fresh parsley
4 teaspoons chopped fresh basil
4 ripe tomatoes

1. Place salami in shallow dish. Pour over combined oil, juice, zest, pepper, garlic, parsley and basil, stand 1 hour, turning once.

2. Cut tomatoes into thick slices. Arrange overlapping slices of tomato and salami on serving plate, pour over remaining oil mixture before serving.
Serves 4 to 6.

__Note:__ Recipe best prepared several hours ahead. Not suitable to freeze.

CAKES, COOKIES & BREADS

Rich and luscious are the famous cakes of Italy. Also delicious, the exotic cookies, many of them with delicious almond flavoring.

RICOTTA CAKE
Torta di Ricotta

YOU WILL NEED
1 package chocolate cake mix
1¼ cups sliced almonds

SYRUP
3 tablespoons superfine sugar
⅓ cup water
3 tablespoons Grand Marnier

FILLING
6oz ricotta cheese
¼ cup superfine sugar
3 tablespoons Grand Marnier
2 tablespoons chopped candied gingerroot
2 tablespoons chopped candied cherries
1oz semisweet chocolate, finely chopped

ICING
¼ cup superfine sugar
⅓ cup water
3oz semisweet chocolate
½ cup (1 stick) butter

1. Grease two 8 inch round baking pans, line base with paper, grease paper. Make up cake mix according to directions on package, spoon mixture into prepared pans. Bake in 350°F oven about 25 minutes or until cakes are cooked when tested. Turn onto wire racks to cool.

2. Place almonds on baking sheet, bake in 350°F oven about 5 minutes or until lightly browned; cool. (This recipe requires only one cake, the remaining cake can be frozen for future use.)

3. Split cake horizontally into 3 layers. Place one layer on serving plate; brush with syrup. Spread half the filling over cake, top with another layer of cake, brush with syrup, spread evenly with remaining filling. Brush remaining layer of cake with syrup, place on filling.

4. Spread cake evenly with icing, press almonds around side of cake. Using a spatula, swirl icing on top. Refrigerate until ready to serve; stand at room temperature 10 minutes before serving.

Syrup: Combine sugar, water and liqueur in pan, stir over heat until sugar is dissolved; cool.

Filling: Push cheese through sieve into bowl. Beat with electric mixer until smooth and creamy. Gradually beat in sugar and liqueur, stir in gingerroot, cherries and chocolate.

Icing: Combine sugar and water in pan, stir over heat until sugar is dissolved, bring to boil; cool. Place chocolate in top half of double saucepan, stir over simmering water until melted. Beat butter in bowl with electric mixer until soft and creamy, gradually beat in cooled syrup, a few drops at a time. Gradually add chocolate, beat well.

Serves 8.

Note: Recipe can be made a day ahead. Not suitable to freeze.

90

FIG & NUT CAKE

Torta di Frutta Secca

YOU WILL NEED
3oz semisweet chocolate
⅔ cup slivered almonds
¼lb dried figs
¼lb candied peel
1 cup roasted hazelnuts
3 eggs
½ cup superfine sugar
1¼ cups self-rising flour

1. Grease a 4 inch x 8 inch loaf pan, line base with paper, grease paper. Finely chop chocolate. Chop almonds, figs, peel and hazelnuts.

2. Beat eggs and sugar in small bowl with electric mixer until pale and fluffy. Fold in chocolate, nuts, figs and peel.

3. Gently fold in sifted flour. Spread mixture into prepared pan. Bake in 350°F oven about 1 hour or until light golden brown and cooked when tested. Cool slightly in pan, turn onto wire rack to cool completely.

Note: *Recipe can be made 2 days ahead. Suitable to freeze.*

SIENA CAKE

Panforte di Siena

YOU WILL NEED
¾ cup whole blanched almonds, chopped
¾ cup roasted hazelnuts, chopped
¼ cup chopped candied apricots
¼ cup chopped candied pineapple
⅓ cup chopped candied peel
⅔ cup all-purpose flour
3 tablespoons unsweetened cocoa powder
1 teaspoon ground cinnamon
2oz semisweet chocolate, chopped
⅓ cup superfine sugar
½ cup honey
confectioners' sugar

From Siena, in the Tuscan region of Italy comes this famous nut cake – so popular that it is exported from its native land to many countries. It is a dense cake and can be cut into slices about ½ inch thick and then into small pieces. It is a perfect accompaniment to after-dinner coffee.

1. Spread almonds on baking sheet, bake in 350°F oven about 5 minutes or until lightly browned. Combine all nuts, apricots, pineapple and peel in bowl. Add sifted flour, cocoa powder and cinnamon; mix well.

2. Grease a deep 8 inch round baking pan, line base with baking paper. Line side of pan with a strip of baking paper, allowing the paper to extend 3 inches above edge of pan.

3. Place chocolate in top half of double saucepan, stir over simmering water until melted. Combine superfine sugar and honey in separate pan, stir over low heat until sugar is dissolved, brushing down sides of pan with brush dipped in hot water to dissolve sugar crystals. Bring to boil, simmer, uncovered, about 5 minutes or until a teaspoon of syrup forms a soft ball when dropped into cold water. Add syrup and melted chocolate to fruit and nut mixture; mix well.

4. Spread mixture quickly and evenly into prepared pan. Bake in 325°F oven 35 minutes, remove from oven; cool in pan. Turn out, remove paper. Wrap in foil. Stand at least 1 day before cutting. Before serving, sift confectioners' sugar thickly over top of cake.

Note: *Recipe can be made 4 weeks ahead. Suitable to freeze. Keep cake wrapped in foil. It is not necessary to refrigerate cake.*

MAMMA'S CAKE

Torta di Mamma

YOU WILL NEED
1 package sponge cake mix
1 cup strong black coffee
⅓ cup coffee liqueur
⅓ cup brandy
4 teaspoons superfine sugar
1 cup whipped cream
unsweetened cocoa powder

FILLING
3oz semisweet chocolate, chopped
¾ cup cornstarch
⅔ cup sugar
2½ cups milk
1½ cups heavy cream
2 tablespoons (¼ stick) butter
2 tablespoons vanilla extract
2 egg yolks, lightly beaten

1. Grease a deep 9 inch round baking pan. Make up sponge cake mix according to directions on package, pour mixture into prepared pan. Bake in 350°F oven about 35 minutes or until cooked. Turn onto wire rack to cool. Combine cold coffee, liqueur, brandy and sugar in bowl; mix well.

2. Split cake into 4 even layers, place first layer onto serving plate; brush with coffee mixture. Spread half vanilla filling evenly over cake. Place second layer on top, brush with coffee mixture; spread one-third chocolate filling over cake. Place a third layer on top of filling, brush with coffee mixture. Spread with remaining half of vanilla filling.

Top with final layer of cake, brush with coffee mixture.

3. Spread remaining chocolate filling evenly over top and side of cake, smooth filling over surface with a large spatula. Refrigerate cake several hours or overnight. Pipe whipped cream around top of cake and dust cake with finely sifted cocoa powder.

Filling: Place chocolate in top half of double saucepan, stir over simmering water until melted; cool slightly. Combine cornstarch and sugar in pan, gradually stir in enough milk to make a smooth paste. Stir in remaining milk and cream. Stir over heat until mixture boils and thickens. Add butter, stir until melted. Remove from heat, add vanilla extract and egg yolks; mix well. Divide filling evenly into 2 bowls. Add melted chocolate to one bowl of filling; mix well. Cover surface with plastic wrap; cool. Cover surface of vanilla filling with plastic wrap; cool. Beat fillings until smooth.

Note: Recipe can be made a day ahead. Not suitable to freeze.

ANISE COOKIES

Biscotti all'Anice

YOU WILL NEED
¾ cup whole blanched almonds
½ cup (1 stick) unsalted butter
¾ cup superfine sugar
3 eggs
3 tablespoons brandy
4 teaspoons grated lemon zest
1½ cups all-purpose flour
¾ cup self-rising flour
4 teaspoons aniseeds

1. Place almonds on baking sheet, bake in 350°F oven about 5 minutes or until lightly browned; cool. Chop roughly.

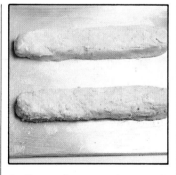

2. Cream butter and sugar in bowl, add eggs 1 at a time, beating well after each addition. Add brandy and zest; mix well. Stir in sifted flours, almonds and aniseeds, cover; refrigerate 1 hour. Halve dough, place on greased baking sheet. Shape into 2 inch x 12 inch logs.

4. Bake in 350°F oven about 20 minutes or until lightly browned; cool on baking sheet. Cut logs diagonally into ½ inch slices with serrated knife. Place slices close together, cut-side-up, on lightly greased baking sheets, bake in 350°F oven about 25 minutes or until dry and crisp; cool. Store in airtight container.
Makes about 40.

Note: Recipe can be made 2 weeks ahead. Suitable to freeze.

FLORENTINES

YOU WILL NEED
¼ cup slivered almonds
¼ cup walnuts
**4 teaspoons chopped
    candied peel**
4 teaspoons golden raisins
5 candied cherries
3 pieces candied gingerroot
¼ cup (½ stick) butter
¼ cup superfine sugar
4 teaspoons heavy cream
**¼lb semisweet chocolate,
    chopped**

From Florence comes this delightful little cookie, the fame of which has spread around the world. They can be made in a smaller size to serve with after-dinner coffee.

1. Finely chop almonds, walnuts, peel, raisins, cherries and gingerroot; combine in bowl. (Or process until finely chopped, transfer to bowl.)

2. Melt butter in small pan, add sugar, stir over gentle heat until all sugar is dissolved. Bring to boil, boil gently over low heat, without stirring, 1 minute; mixture should be just beginning to turn light golden.
    Add butter mixture and cream to fruit and nut mixture; mix well.

3. Spoon heaped teaspoons of mixture onto greased baking sheets about 2 inches apart. For easy handling, it is best to bake 4 at a time.

4. Bake in 350°F oven about 10 minutes or until golden brown. Remove from oven, using spatula, push each Florentine into a round shape. Cool on baking sheets 1 minute. Using spatula, carefully lift onto wire rack to cool.

5. Place chocolate in top half of double saucepan, stir over simmering water until melted; cool slightly. Spread 1 teaspoon of chocolate on underside of each Florentine. When chocolate is almost set, run a fork through chocolate to give a wavy effect. Place on baking sheet, refrigerate until chocolate is set. Store in airtight container until required.

Makes about 20.

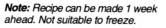

Note: *Recipe can be made 1 week ahead. Not suitable to freeze.*

98

ALMOND COOKIES

YOU WILL NEED
1 egg white
¼ cup superfine sugar
4 teaspoons honey
1 teaspoon grated lemon zest
2 cups packaged ground almonds
4 teaspoons self-rising flour
1 egg white, lightly beaten, extra

TOPPING
½ cup superfine sugar
¼ teaspoon vanilla extract

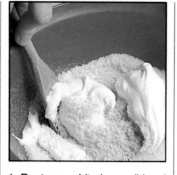

1. Beat egg white in small bowl until soft peaks form, gradually add sugar and honey, beat until sugar is dissolved between additions. Add zest, almonds and sifted flour; mix well.

2. Shape tablespoons of mixture into 2 inch lengths, place onto greased baking sheets. Bake in 325°F oven about 40 minutes or until lightly browned. Remove from oven.

3. Reserve 2 teaspoons of extra egg white for topping. Brush tops of cookies with remaining egg white. Press a teaspoon of topping onto warm cookies with a spoon. The topping will harden on cooling. Store in airtight container.
Topping: Combine reserved egg white, sugar and vanilla extract in bowl.

Makes about 16.

Note: Recipe can be made 1 week ahead. Suitable to freeze.

AMARETTI

YOU WILL NEED
1 cup ground almonds
1 cup sugar
2 large egg whites
½ teaspoon vanilla extract
1 or 2 drops almond extract
whole blanched almonds

1. Combine ground almonds, sugar, unbeaten egg whites, vanilla extract and almond extract in small bowl; mix well.

2. Beat with electric mixer on medium speed 3 minutes; stand 5 minutes.

3. Lightly grease baking sheets, dust with flour, shake away excess flour. Spoon almond mixture into piping bag fitted with ½ inch plain tube. Pipe mixture on baking sheets to make cookies about 1½ inches in diameter (they can be smaller). Top with a whole blanched almond or almond half. Stand amaretti, uncovered, at room temperature overnight.

Bake in 350°F oven about 12 minutes or until tops are lightly browned; stand 5 minutes before lifting with a metal spatula onto wire rack to cool.

Makes about 20.

Note: Recipe can be made a week ahead. Not suitable to freeze. Coarsely ground almonds will give better results in amaretti than finely ground almonds.

SICILIAN CREAMS

Biscotti alla Siciliana

YOU WILL NEED
1¾ cups self-rising flour
¼ cup (½ stick) butter
½ cup superfine sugar
1 teaspoon grated lemon zest
1 teaspoon vanilla extract
1 egg, lightly beaten
¼ cup milk
4 teaspoons water
4 teaspoons liqueur (see note)
whipped cream
confectioners' sugar

1. Sift flour into bowl, rub in butter, add superfine sugar; mix well. Make well in center, add combined zest, vanilla extract, egg and milk, mix with wooden spoon to a soft, pliable dough.

2. Turn dough onto lightly floured surface, knead gently until smooth; dough should be soft and pliable. Roll dough out until ½ inch thick, cut into 2 inch rounds using cutter. Place rounds on lightly greased baking sheets, about 1 inch apart. Bake in 350°F oven about 15 minutes or until lightly browned; cool on wire rack.

3. Cut cold cookies in half using a fine serrated knife, brush underside of tops with combined water and liqueur. Sandwich cookies with whipped cream, dust with sifted confectioners' sugar.

Makes about 12.

Note: Cookies can be made a day ahead. Cut and fill close to serving. Unfilled cookies suitable to freeze. Any liqueur can be used, e.g. Galliano, Grand Marnier, Cointreau, Amaretto.

PAGNOTTA

YOU WILL NEED
1 package (¼oz) dry active yeast
½ cup lukewarm water
½ teaspoon sugar
3 cups all-purpose flour
1 teaspoon salt
4 teaspoons olive oil
1 cup lukewarm water, extra
all-purpose flour, extra

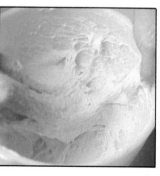

1. Combine yeast, warm water and sugar in bowl, cover, stand in warm place about 15 minutes or until mixture is foamy. Sift flour and salt into bowl, make well in center, stir in yeast mixture, oil and extra water. Mix with hand, beating dough well, until dough begins to leave side of bowl.

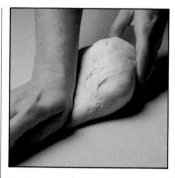

2. Place dough in large oiled bowl, cover, stand in warm place about 30 minutes or until doubled in size. Turn dough onto lightly floured surface, knead well 5 minutes, using as little flour as possible.

3. Shape dough into a round, place on lightly greased baking sheet, dust top thickly with sifted extra flour. Cut top as shown, making cut about 1 inch deep. Place loaf into cold oven, turn temperature to 375°F, bake about 45 minutes or until loaf is browned and sounds hollow when tapped on the base.

Note: Recipe can be made 2 days ahead, although it is best eaten fresh on day of baking. Suitable to freeze.

ALMOND CAKE

Dolce di Mandorle

YOU WILL NEED
4 large eggs
⅓ cup superfine sugar
1 teaspoon grated lemon zest
⅓ cup all-purpose flour
¼ cup cornstarch
¼ cup packaged ground almonds
2 tablespoons (¼ stick) butter, melted
1½ cups red currant jelly
¾ cup sliced almonds

TOPPING
3 cups (¾lb) packaged ground almonds
⅓ cup superfine sugar
6 large eggs, separated
½ cup rum

2. Split cake evenly into 3 layers. Place 1 layer on baking sheet, spread with ⅓ cup of the jelly, top with another layer of cake, spread with ⅓ cup of jelly, top with final layer of cake. Spread the larger portion of topping evenly around side and top of cake. If mixture is hard to spread, add more egg white.

1. Grease a deep 8 inch round baking pan, dust with flour, shake away excess flour. Combine eggs, sugar and zest in small bowl of electric mixer. Beat on high speed until mixture is thick and frothy and fills bowl. Gently fold in sifted flour, cornstarch and almonds, fold in butter. Pour mixture into prepared pan. Bake in 350˚F oven about 30 minutes or until cooked. Turn cake onto wire rack to cool; stand overnight.

3. Spoon reserved topping into piping bag fitted with a fluted tube. Pipe in a zig-zag pattern over top of cake; pipe small rosettes around edge of cake. Bake cake in 475˚F oven about 8 minutes or until side of cake turns white and rosettes are lightly browned. Remove cake from oven immediately. Melt remaining jelly in pan, spoon some of the jelly between zig-zag design; stand 10 minutes. Spread side of cake with remaining jelly, press sliced almonds onto jelly; cool.
Topping: Combine almonds and sugar in bowl, gradually stir in combined egg yolks and rum; mix well. Combine 3 tablespoons of egg white with one-third of the topping; reserve. Add 4 teaspoons egg white to remaining topping; mix well.

Note: Recipe can be made a day ahead. Not suitable to freeze. Keep remaining egg white for another recipe.

COCONUT COOKIES

Biscotti al Cocco

YOU WILL NEED
2 large egg yolks
¼ cup superfine sugar
2 cups shredded coconut
1 large egg white

1. Beat egg yolks and sugar in bowl with electric mixer until creamy, stir in coconut.

2. Beat egg white in separate bowl until firm peaks form, gently fold into coconut mixture.

3. Drop teaspoons of mixture onto greased baking sheets. Bake in 300°F oven 15 minutes, reduce heat to 250°F, bake further 30 minutes or until cookies are golden brown. Makes about 18.

Note: *Recipe can be made a week ahead. Suitable to freeze.*

CANNOLI

YOU WILL NEED
3 cups all-purpose flour
3 egg yolks
1 egg, lightly beaten
1 teaspoon grated lemon zest
¼ cup marsala
24 cannelloni pasta tubes
1 egg white, lightly beaten
oil for deep-frying
confectioners' sugar, extra
2oz semisweet chocolate, grated

FILLING
2lb ricotta cheese
1½ cups confectioners' sugar
6 x 2in cinnamon sticks
1 teaspoon grated lemon zest
¼ cup chopped candied peel

1. Sift 1 cup of the flour into bowl, rub in egg yolks. Refrigerate 2 hours. Add remaining flour, egg, zest and marsala; mix well. Turn onto lightly floured surface, knead 15 minutes. Cover, refrigerate 1 hour.

2. Cut pastry into 4 pieces. Roll out each piece on lightly floured surface until paper thin. (This is important; if the pastry is too thick, it will not be crisp and have the characteristic "bubbles", when deep-fried.) If you have a pasta machine, roll pastry through 3 times, adjusting the machine to roll pastry thinner each time. Measure the length of the cannelloni tubes, then cut pastry into strips about ¼ inch narrower than tubes. Place tube at one end of pastry, roll pastry around, then cut so that about ½ inch overlaps.

    Brush edge with egg white, press firmly into position. Do not brush egg white on cannelloni tube or it will be hard to remove. Cut remaining strips of pastry the same size.

3. Deep-fry cannoli, 4 at a time, in hot oil until golden brown, drain on absorbent paper; cool 1 minute. Using a clean kitchen towel, carefully remove cannelloni tube from inside cannoli; discard tube. Cool pastry shells completely; they become crisp on cooling. Spoon filling into large piping bag fitted with a plain tube. Pipe filling into cannoli shells. Roll cannoli in sifted confectioners' sugar, dip ends in chocolate.

Filling: Beat cheese and sifted sugar in bowl with electric mixer on high speed 5 minutes. Blend cinnamon sticks about 1 minute or until powdery; you will need 3 tablespoons of cinnamon. Add cinnamon, zest and peel to cheese, beat further 3 minutes. Makes about 24.

Note: *Cannoli shells can be made 2 days ahead. Fill just before serving. Not suitable to freeze. There are metal cannoli molds available but we found cannelloni pasta tubes make excellent molds.*

DESSERTS

The finale for an Italian family meal is generally fruit or cheese, but mouth-watering desserts are prepared for special occasions.

ZUPPA INGLESE

YOU WILL NEED
6 eggs
1¼ cups superfine sugar
1 cup all-purpose flour
½ cup cornstarch
1½ teaspoons double-acting baking powder
⅔ cup milk
3 tablespoons rum
1lb strawberries
2½ cups whipping cream
2 teaspoons sugar
3 tablespoons strawberry jam
4 teaspoons rum, extra

FILLING
¾ cup cornstarch
⅔ cup sugar
2½ cups milk
1¼ cups heavy cream
2 tablespoons (¼ stick) butter
2 tablespoons vanilla extract
4 egg yolks, lightly beaten

This is the famous dessert cake of Italy, made for birthdays and celebrations or just for a delicious treat. Literally translated, the name means "English soup"; it is a rum-flavored cake thought to have acquired the unusual name because of the association of English sailors and their issue of rum. It makes an impressive party dessert and gives 10 to 12 servings.

1. Grease a deep 11 inch round baking pan. Beat eggs in bowl with electric mixer until thick and creamy, gradually add sugar, beat until dissolved. Fold in sifted dry ingredients. Pour mixture into prepared pan. Bake in 350˚F oven about 35 minutes or until cooked. Cool on wire rack.

2. Split cake evenly into 3 layers. Place one layer of cake into cleaned baking pan. Brush with combined milk and rum. Spread with half the filling. Reserve 8 strawberries. Slice remaining strawberries. Sprinkle half the sliced strawberries over filling. Place second layer of cake on top, brush with rum mixture. Spread with remaining filling, sprinkle with remaining sliced strawberries. Top with final layer of cake, brush with remaining rum mixture. Cover, refrigerate overnight.

3. Turn cake onto serving plate. Beat cream and sugar in small bowl until soft peaks form. Spread two-thirds of cream over cake. Spoon remaining cream into piping bag fitted with a star tube, pipe around cake. Heat jam and extra rum in pan; strain. Brush reserved strawberries with jam mixture, place on cake.

Filling: Combine cornstarch and sugar in pan, gradually stir in enough milk to make a smooth paste. Stir in remaining milk and cream. Stir over heat until mixture boils and thickens; remove from heat. Add butter, stir until melted. Stir in vanilla extract and egg yolks; mix well. Place filling in bowl, cover surface with plastic wrap; cool. Beat cold filling until smooth.

Note: Recipe best prepared a day ahead. Not suitable to freeze.

CHOCOLATE CREAM PUFFS

Bignè alla Cioccolata

YOU WILL NEED
1 cup hot water
½ cup (1 stick) butter
1 cup all-purpose flour
4 large eggs
2 teaspoons unsweetened cocoa powder, extra
⅓ cup unsweetened cocoa powder, extra
⅓ cup superfine sugar
PASTRY CREAM
2 egg yolks
¼ cup superfine sugar
1 tablespoon all-purpose flour
⅔ cup heavy cream
¼ teaspoon vanilla extract
1 cup (2 sticks) unsalted butter
3 tablespoons superfine sugar, extra
1oz semisweet chocolate, melted

1. Combine water and butter in pan, stir over heat until butter is melted and mixture boils. Add sifted flour all at once, stir rapidly over heat until mixture forms a ball and leaves side of pan; cool slightly. Place mixture in small bowl of electric mixer, add eggs 1 at a time, beating well after each addition. Beat in sifted cocoa powder. Place teaspoons of mixture on lightly greased baking sheets, allowing room for spreading. Bake in 400°F oven 10 minutes, reduce heat to 350°F, bake further 40 minutes or until puffs are crisp. Cut small slits in side of each puff to allow steam to escape; return puffs to oven 5 minutes to dry out; cool. Remove any soft dough from inside puffs using a small spoon.

2. Spoon pastry cream into piping bag fitted with small plain tube, pipe into puffs.

3. Combine sifted extra cocoa powder and sugar in bowl, roll puffs in mixture to coat all over. Keep in refrigerator until ready to serve.

Pastry Cream: Beat egg yolks and sugar in small bowl with electric mixer until pale. Reduce speed to low, add sifted flour, cream and vanilla extract. Place mixture in pan, stir over heat until mixture boils, boil 30 seconds. Remove from heat, beat until smooth; cool. Push mixture through fine sieve to remove any small lumps.

Beat butter in small bowl with electric mixer until soft and creamy, gradually add extra sugar, beat well. Beat in cream mixture, beat until mixture is smooth and almost double in size. Beat in cooled chocolate.

Makes about 36.

Note: Puffs can be made 3 days ahead. Pastry cream can be made a day ahead. On day of serving, recrisp puffs in 300°F oven 5 minutes before filling. Unfilled puffs suitable to freeze.

ZUCCOTTO

YOU WILL NEED
8in round sponge cake layer
3 tablespoons brandy
3 tablespoons Maraschino liqueur
⅓ cup whole blanched almonds
3oz semisweet chocolate, chopped
1¼ cups whipping cream
¼ cup confectioners' sugar
½ cup roasted hazelnuts, chopped

1. Cut cake into ½ inch thick slices; reserve 3 slices. Cut each slice diagonally, making 2 triangles. Carefully brush one side of each cake triangle with combined brandy and liqueur. Line 5 cup pudding steamer or bowl with a layer of damp muslin. Place cake triangles, unbrushed-side-down, in steamer, having narrow ends on the base. Repeat until steamer is completely lined with cake triangles. Fill any gaps with pieces of cake. Trim cake level with top of steamer. Reserve remaining cake triangles and pieces.

2. Place almonds on baking sheet, bake in 350°F oven about 5 minutes or until lightly browned; cool. Roughly chop almonds. Reserve 1oz of chocolate. Place remaining chocolate in top half of double saucepan, stir over simmering water until melted. Beat cream and sifted sugar in bowl until soft peaks form, fold in nuts. Divide mix-ture in half, fold reserved chocolate into one half, spread evenly over cake in steamer. Stir melted chocolate into remaining cream mixture, spoon mixture into steamer, pressing in firmly.

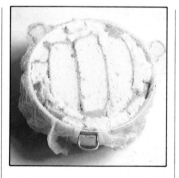

3. Brush reserved cake slices with leftover brandy mixture, arrange over chocolate mixture, filling any gaps with reserved cake triangles and pieces. Cover, refrigerate overnight. Turn zucotto carefully onto serving plate. If desired, dust top with sifted confectioners' sugar and cocoa powder.

Serves 6.

This is a special dessert from Florence. The shape of the dessert is said to resemble the dome of Florence's famous church, the Duomo.

Note: Recipe can be made 2 days ahead. Not suitable to freeze. Any liqueur can be used in this recipe.

ST JOSEPH'S DAY PASTRIES

Sfinci di san Giuseppe

YOU WILL NEED
1 cup water
3oz (¾ stick) butter
1 cup all-purpose flour
4 eggs

FILLING
⅔ cup cornstarch
⅓ cup sugar
2 cups milk
1½ cups heavy cream
1 tablespoon vanilla extract
3 egg yolks, lightly beaten
1 teaspoon grated
   orange zest
1 teaspoon grated
   lemon zest
3 tablespoons Amaretto
   liqueur

CHOCOLATE SAUCE
¼lb semisweet chocolate,
   chopped
1 egg yolk
¼ cup fresh orange juice
1 teaspoon grated
   orange zest
3 tablespoons Amaretto
   liqueur
1 teaspoon cornstarch
4 teaspoons water
½ cup heavy cream

Italian pastrycooks created these treats to commemorate St Joseph's Day, March 16. He is the patron saint of home and family. Traditionally, the pastries are served plain but we have added a rich, liqueur-flavored chocolate sauce.

1. Place water and butter in pan, stir over heat until butter is melted. Bring to boil, add sifted flour all at once, stir over heat until mixture forms a ball and leaves side of pan. Remove from heat; cool slightly.

2. Place mixture into small bowl of electric mixer, add eggs 1 at a time, beating mixture well after each addition.

3. Drop rounded tablespoons of mixture onto greased baking sheets, allowing room for spreading. Bake in 400°F oven 10 minutes. Reduce heat to 350°F, bake further 40 minutes or until puffs are crisp. Make a small slit in sides of puffs to allow steam to escape; bake further 5 minutes to dry out; cool on wire rack.

4. Pipe filling into puffs, arrange on plates, pour hot chocolate sauce over puffs.

Filling: Combine cornstarch and sugar in pan, gradually stir in enough milk to make a smooth paste. Stir in remaining milk and cream, stir over heat until mixture boils and thickens. Remove from heat, add vanilla extract, egg yolks, zest and liqueur; mix well. Place filling in bowl, cover surface with plastic wrap; cool. Beat until smooth.

Chocolate Sauce: Combine chocolate, egg yolk, juice and zest in top half of double saucepan. Stir over simmering water until smooth and slightly thickened, add liqueur; cool. Stir in blended cornstarch and water, stir over direct heat until sauce boils and thickens. Add cream, reheat without boiling.

Makes about 12.

Note: Puffs can be made 3 days ahead. Just before serving, crisp in 300°F oven 5 minutes and fill. Filling can be made 2 days ahead. Sauce best made on day of serving. Unfilled puffs suitable to freeze. Any favorite liqueur can be used in this recipe.

APPLE CREAM PIE

Torta di Mele alla Panna

YOU WILL NEED
1¼ cups all-purpose flour
½ teaspoon ground cinnamon
1 teaspoon double-acting baking powder
¼ cup superfine sugar
2 teaspoons grated lemon zest
½ cup (1 stick) butter
1 egg yolk, lightly beaten
3 tablespoons dry sherry
2 green apples, peeled
1 teaspoon ground cinnamon, extra
1¼ cups whipping cream

FILLING
2 eggs
½ cup sugar
3 tablespoons all-purpose flour
2 teaspoons grated lemon zest
½ cup heavy cream
8oz package cream cheese, softened
4 teaspoons candied peel
¼ cup chopped dark seedless raisins

1. Sift dry ingredients into bowl, add zest, rub in butter. Add combined egg yolk and sherry, mix to a firm dough, press mixture into a ball.

2. Roll out pastry until large enough to line shallow 7 inch x 11 inch baking pan, lift into pan; trim edges.

3. Quarter cored apples, slice thinly. Arrange in pastry base as shown. Pour filling over apples. Bake in 350°F oven 1¼ hours. To serve warm, sprinkle with extra cinnamon, serve with cream. To serve cold, stand until cold, spread with cream, sprinkle with extra cinnamon.
Filling: Beat eggs and sugar in bowl until thick, gradually add sifted flour, zest, cream, cheese, peel and raisins; mix well.
Serves 6.

Note: Recipe can be made a day ahead. Not suitable to freeze.

SICILIAN CHEESECAKE

Cassata Siciliana

YOU WILL NEED
6oz plain chocolate cookies, crushed
3oz (¾ stick) butter, melted
½ cup whipping cream, whipped
2oz semisweet chocolate, grated

FILLING
1¼lb ricotta cheese
1 cup confectioners' sugar
1 teaspoon vanilla extract
3 tablespoons Creme de Cacao liqueur
2oz semisweet chocolate
3 tablespoons chopped candied fruit

1. Combine cookies and butter in bowl; mix well. Press mixture evenly over base of 8 inch springform pan. Refrigerate while preparing filling.

2. Spoon filling into pan, spread evenly, refrigerate overnight or at least 6 hours. Spread cream over top of cake, sprinkle edge with chocolate.

Filling: Combine cheese, sifted sugar, vanilla extract and liqueur in small bowl, beat until smooth and fluffy. Grate chocolate, stir into cheese mixture with fruit; mix well.

Note: Recipe can be made 2 days ahead. Not suitable to freeze. Any mixture of candied fruits can be used in this recipe.

GLAZED ORANGES

YOU WILL NEED
4 oranges
1¼ cups sugar
1½ cups water
¼ cup water, extra
3 tablespoons Grand
**   Marnier liqueur**
2 teaspoons fresh lemon
**   juice**

1. Using a vegetable peeler, cut strips of peel thinly from 2 oranges. Remove any white pith from strips. Cut into thin strips.

2. Peel all oranges, removing white pith. Cut oranges horizontally into 4 slices for easy serving. Reassemble oranges, secure with wooden skewers.

3. Place peel strips in pan, cover with water, boil, uncovered, 10 minutes; drain. Combine sugar and water in pan, stir over heat until sugar is dissolved; add peel strips. Boil gently, uncovered, about 10 minutes or until strips are transparent and glazed. Remove strips from syrup, place on oiled plate.

4. Boil syrup, uncovered, further 5 minutes or until syrup turns pale golden brown. Remove from heat, quickly add extra water (mixture will crackle), stir to dissolve any toffee in base of pan. Stand 5 minutes, stir in liqueur and juice; cool.

Pour syrup over oranges, add glazed peel strips, cover; refrigerate several hours or overnight. Remove skewers from glazed oranges just before serving. Serve oranges topped with peel strips and drizzled with toffee syrup.

Serves 4.

Note: *Recipe can be made 2 days ahead. Not suitable to freeze. It is important to remove white pith from oranges as it is quite bitter and will adversely affect the taste.*

ZABAGLIONE

YOU WILL NEED
5 egg yolks
¼ cup superfine sugar
½ cup marsala
¼ cup dry white wine

1. Combine egg yolks and sugar in top half of double saucepan. Beat with hand beater or electric mixer until well combined.

2. Place over simmering water. Gradually beat in half the marsala and half the white wine; beat well. Gradually beat in remaining marsala and wine.

3. Beat constantly about 10 minutes or until thick and creamy. If mixture adheres to side of pan, quickly remove from simmering water, beat vigorously with wooden spoon – especially around base of pan. Pour into individual dishes.

Serves 4.

Note: *Recipe best made just before serving. Not suitable to freeze. Any favorite liqueur can be used. Zabaglione makes an excellent topping for fresh fruit, and is also delicious served warm over ice cream.*

CASSATA

YOU WILL NEED
2 eggs, separated
½ cup confectioners' sugar
½ cup whipping cream
few drops almond extract

CHOCOLATE LAYER
2 eggs, separated
½ cup confectioners' sugar
½ cup whipping cream
2oz semisweet chocolate, melted
3 tablespoons unsweetened cocoa powder
2 tablespoons water

FRUIT LAYER
1 cup whipping cream
1 teaspoon vanilla extract
1 egg white
⅓ cup confectioners' sugar
⅓ cup sliced almonds, toasted
3 tablespoons red candied cherries, chopped
2 candied apricots, chopped
2 candied pineapple rings, chopped
1 tablespoon green candied cherries, chopped

Beat egg whites in small bowl until firm peaks form, gradually beat in sifted sugar. Fold in lightly beaten egg yolks. Beat cream and almond extract in separate bowl until soft peaks form, fold into egg mixture. Pour into deep 8 inch round baking pan. Smooth top, freeze until firm.

Pour chocolate layer into pan; freeze until firm. Pour fruit layer into pan; freeze until firm. Stand cassata 10 minutes at room temperature. Run a spatula around edge of cassata, turn onto plate. Cut into wedges.

Chocolate Layer: Beat egg whites in small bowl until firm peaks form, gradually beat in sifted sugar. Beat cream in separate bowl until soft peaks form, fold into egg white mixture. Combine chocolate and egg yolks in bowl; stir in combined cocoa powder and water. Fold chocolate mixture gently into cream mixture.

Fruit Layer: Beat cream and vanilla extract in small bowl until firm peaks form. Beat egg white in separate bowl until soft peaks form, gradually add sifted sugar, beat well after each addition. Stir egg white mixture, almonds and fruit into cream mixture.

Serves 6 to 8.

Note: Recipe can be made 1 week ahead. Serve with whipped cream and fresh fruit, if desired.

LEMON GELATO

Gelato al Limone

YOU WILL NEED
½ cup superfine sugar
½ cup water
½ cup sweet or dry white wine
½ cup fresh lemon juice
1 egg white

1. Combine sugar, water and wine in small pan, stir over heat until sugar is dissolved, simmer, uncovered, 10 minutes; cool.

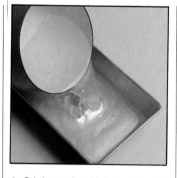

2. Stir in strained juice; mix well. Pour mixture into shallow pan, freeze about 1 hour or until mixture is just firm.

3. Turn mixture into bowl, beat with fork until smooth. Beat egg white in separate bowl until soft peaks form, fold into gelato mixture. Return to pan, freeze until firm.

Serves 2.

Note: Recipe can be made 1 week ahead. This gelato will serve 4 if served with fresh fruit.

...AND SOMETHING EXTRA

Just a little something extra to end the book – unusual recipes, both sweet and savory.

MUSTARD FRUITS

Mostarda di Frutta

YOU WILL NEED
1 pear
1 apple
1 orange
2oz green grapes
2oz black grapes
16½oz can black cherries
2 tablespoons candied peel
10 whole cloves
cinnamon sticks
¾ cup red wine vinegar
¾ cup water
¾ cup sugar
2 teaspoons dry mustard

These are a specialty of Cremona in Lombardy. They're rather like a fresh fruit relish and they make an excellent accompaniment to meat. When in season, other fruits – peaches, apricots, etc. – can be used.

There are three methods used to sterilize jars.
1. Place jars in dishwasher, use rinse cycle and hottest temperature; do not add detergent.
2. Place clean jars in a large pan, cover with cold water, cover pan, bring to boil; boil 20 minutes. Remove jars from water; drain well, stand right way up on a clean wooden board.
3. Wash jars well in hot soapy water, rinse thoroughly in hot water. Stand jars rightway up on baking sheet, place in 300°F oven 30 minutes.

1. Peel and core pear and apple, cut into quarters; cut into thick slices. Peel orange, cut into thick slices; cut slices in half. Remove grapes from stalks, wash and pat dry. Drain cherries. Place pear, apple, orange, grapes and cherries in large bowl, add peel and cloves, toss gently. Pack fruit mixture into hot, sterilized jars. Add a cinnamon stick to each jar.

2. Combine vinegar, water and sugar in pan, stir over heat until sugar is dissolved. Boil, uncovered, 5 minutes. Add mustard, stir until combined. Pour syrup over fruit to cover completely, seal while hot; cool. Refrigerate fruits 1 week before using, keep refrigerated after opening jar.

Makes about 4 cups.

Note: *Recipe can be made 4 weeks ahead. Not suitable to freeze.*

ALMOND CRUNCH

Mandorlata

YOU WILL NEED
1¾ cups sugar
3 tablespoons fresh lemon juice
1 cup whole blanched almonds
¼ cup honey
1¼ cups heavy cream

1. Lightly oil a marble slab or baking sheet. Combine ½ cup of the sugar and juice in large pan. Stir over heat until sugar is dissolved. Boil, without stirring, about 6 minutes or until mixture turns dark golden brown. Remove from heat, add almonds; mix well. Drop mixture onto prepared marble slab; cool.

2. Oil a shallow 7 inch x 11 inch baking pan. Place remaining sugar, honey and cream in large heavy pan, stir over heat until sugar is dissolved. Stir until mixture comes to the boil, boil without stirring, until a teaspoon of mixture dropped into a cup of cold water forms a hard ball between the fingers (260°F on candy thermometer). This will take about 30 minutes. Do not allow mixture to boil over. While mixture is boiling, break almond toffee into pieces, blend or process until fine.

3. Quickly stir processed almond toffee into cream mixture, pour into prepared pan; cool slightly. Using knife, mark into 1 inch squares; stand until cold. Cut into squares when cold.

Note: *Recipe can be made 1 week ahead. Not suitable to freeze. For best results, use a candy thermometer.*

ALMOND NOUGAT

Torrone

YOU WILL NEED
2 cups sugar
1 cup liquid glucose
½ cup honey
¼ cup water
2 egg whites
1 teaspoon vanilla extract
½ cup (1 stick) butter, chopped
⅓ cup whole blanched almonds, toasted

1. Oil a shallow 7 inch x 11 inch baking pan. Have butter at room temperature. Combine sugar, glucose, honey and water in pan, stir over low heat until sugar is dissolved. Boil, uncovered until a teaspoon of mixture dropped into a cup of cold water forms a hard ball between the fingers (260°F on candy thermometer). This takes about 8 minutes.

2. Beat egg whites in bowl with electric mixer until stiff peaks form. While motor is operating, pour in one-quarter of hot syrup, beating constantly. Continue beating about 5 minutes or until mixture is thick enough to hold its shape; photograph above shows consistency of mixture. Continue boiling remaining syrup about 5 minutes or until a small amount of syrup forms brittle threads when dropped into cold water (310°F on candy thermometer). Pour hot syrup over meringue in a thin stream, beating constantly until mixture is very thick.

3. Add vanilla extract and butter, beat about 5 minutes or until mixture becomes thick. Stir in almonds using wooden spoon. Turn mixture into prepared pan, smooth top with spatula. Refrigerate until firm. Loosen edges of nougat, turn onto board. Using sharp knife, cut nougat into 1½ inch x 1 inch pieces. Wrap each piece in cellulose paper or baking paper. Store in refrigerator.

Makes about 2lb.

Note: *Recipe can be made 1 week ahead. Not suitable to freeze. If desired, ¼lb chopped Turkish Delight can be folded in with the almonds. This gives the pretty pink squares as in the photograph. For best results, use a candy thermometer.*

FRITTATA

YOU WILL NEED
½ cup olive oil
5 onions, finely sliced
14½oz can tomatoes,
    drained, chopped
3 slices cooked ham,
    finely chopped
4 teaspoons chopped
    fresh parsley
½ teaspoon dried basil
    leaves
3 tablespoons grated fresh
    Parmesan cheese
6 eggs, lightly beaten
2 tablespoons (¼ stick)
    butter

1. Heat oil in large skillet, add onions, cook, stirring, until golden brown. Stir in tomatoes, cook, stirring, 5 minutes; cool.

2. Combine onion mixture, ham, parsley, basil, cheese and eggs in bowl; mix well.

3. Heat butter in skillet; while butter is still frothing, pour in egg mixture, spread evenly. Cook over very low heat about 10 minutes or until set and browned underneath. Cook under heated broiler until frittata is set in the center, but not browned. Serve frittata with salad, if desired.
Serves 4.

Note: Recipe best made just before serving. Not suitable to freeze. Reserve tomato liquid for another recipe.

CROSTINI

YOU WILL NEED
12 slices white bread
2 tablespoons (¼ stick)
    butter, melted
3 tablespoons butter, extra
3 tablespoons all-purpose
    flour
1 cup milk
3 tablespoons grated fresh
    Parmesan cheese
3oz button mushrooms,
    finely chopped
2 teaspoons anchovy paste
3 tablespoons grated fresh
    Parmesan cheese, extra
2oz can rolled fillets
    anchovies, drained
3 pitted black olives, sliced
3 pitted green olives, sliced
¼ red or green bell pepper,
    thinly sliced

1. Cut 2 inch rounds of bread using cutter, brush with butter, place on baking sheet. Bake in 350°F oven about 10 minutes or until golden brown; cool.

2. Melt extra butter in pan, add flour, cook, stirring, 1 minute. Remove from heat, gradually add milk, stir over heat until mixture boils and thickens; remove from heat. Add cheese, mushrooms and paste; mix well.

3. Spread 2 teaspoons of mixture over each bread round, top with extra cheese. Top with anchovies, olives or pepper strips. Bake in 400°F oven about 5 minutes or until lightly browned and heated through.
Makes about 24.

Note: Crostini rounds and mushroom topping can be made a day ahead. Assemble crostini just before baking. Crostini rounds suitable to freeze.

GLOSSARY

Here are some names, terms and alternatives to help you understand and use our recipes perfectly.

ALCOHOL: is optional but gives special flavor. Fruit juice, water or broth can be used to make up the liquid content of recipes.

ALMONDS:

Ground: we used packaged commercially ground nuts unless otherwise specified.

Sliced: sliced blanched almonds.

Slivered: thin pieces of blanched almonds.

AMARETTO: almond-flavored liqueur.

ARROWROOT: used mostly for thickening. Cornstarch can be substituted.

BACCALA: salted, dried fillets of cod.

BOUILLON CUBES: available in beef, chicken or vegetable flavors. If preferred, instant bouillon can be used; 1 teaspoon instant bouillon is equivalent to 1 small bouillon cube. Or alternatively, homemade broth can be used; see recipes on page 127. Substitute water and bouillon cube in recipes with broth.

BREAD CRUMBS:

Fresh: use 1 or 2 day-old-bread made into crumbs by grating, blending or processing.

Packaged unseasoned: use fine packaged unseasoned bread crumbs.

BUTTER: use salted or unsalted butter.

CANDIED PEEL: a mixture of candied citrus peel.

CHEESE:

Cream cheese: unripened, smooth spreadable cheese.

Mozzarella: a fresh, semi-soft cheese with a delicate, clean, fresh curd taste, has a low melting point and stringy texture when heated.

Parmesan: sharp-tasting cheese used as a flavor accent. We prefer to use fresh Parmesan cheese, although it is available finely grated.

CHILIES: are available in many different types and sizes. The small ones (birds' eye or bird peppers) are the hottest. Use tight rubber gloves when chopping fresh chilies as they can burn your skin. The seeds are the hottest part of the chilies so remove them if you want to reduce the heat content of recipes.

COINTREAU: orange-flavored liqueur.

CORNMEAL, YELLOW: ground corn (maize), darker and coarser than regular cornmeal. One cannot be substituted for the other as cooking times will vary.

CREAM:

Heavy: a cream with about 35 percent fat content.

Whipping: is specified when necessary in recipes, heavy cream can be substituted.

CREME DE CASSIS: a black-currant flavored liqueur.

CURRY POWDER: a combination of spices in powdered form; consists of chili, coriander, cumin, fennel, fenugreek and turmeric in varying proportions.

DOUBLE-ACTING BAKING POWDER: is a raising agent consisting of an alkali and an acid. It is mostly made from cream of tartar and baking soda in the proportions of 1 level teaspoon cream of tartar to ½ level teaspoon baking soda. This is equivalent to 2 teaspoons baking powder.

FENNEL: has a slight aniseed taste when fresh, ground or in seed form. Fennel seeds are a component of curry powder.

FLOUR:

Self-rising: substitute all-purpose flour and double-acting baking powder in the proportion of 1 cup all-purpose flour to 2 level teaspoons double-acting baking powder. Sift together several times before using.

GALLIANO: a clear, yellow-colored Italian liqueur made from an infusion of various herbs and flowers.

GINGERROOT:

Fresh: scrape away skin and grate, chop or slice gingerroot as required. Fresh, peeled gingerroot can be preserved in jar with enough dry sherry to cover; keep in refrigerator; it will keep for months.

Candied: fresh gingerroot preserved in sugar syrup. Crystallized gingerroot can be substituted; rinse off the sugar with warm water, dry gingerroot before using.

GLUCOSE SYRUP (liquid glucose): is clear with a consistency like honey; it is made from wheat starch; available at natural food stores and supermarkets. Do not confuse it with a glucose drink.

GOLDEN RAISINS: seedless white raisins.

GRAND MARNIER: an orange-flavored liqueur.

GREEN ONIONS: Also known as scallions.

HERBS: we have specified when to use fresh or dried herbs. We used dried (not ground) herbs in the proportion of 1:4 for fresh herbs, for example, 1 teaspoon dried herbs instead of 4 teaspoons chopped fresh herbs.

MARASCHINO: liqueur made from fermented maraschino cherries with added sweeteners; it is used in many cakes and puddings.

MARSALA: a sweet fortified wine.

OLIVE OIL: we used a virgin olive oil but use the grade you prefer. Olive oil comes in several different grades with each grade having a different flavor. The most flavorsome is the extra virgin variety usually used in homemade dressings. Extra virgin olive oil is the purest quality virgin oil. Virgin oil is obtained only from the pulp and kernels of second grade olives. Light olive oil is lightest in color and flavor and is ideal for all-purpose cooking.

PANCETTA: cured pork belly; bacon can be substituted.

PROSCIUTTO: uncooked, unsmoked ham, cured in salt, ready to eat when bought. Usually sliced very finely.

RUM: we used an underproof dark rum.

SAFFRON: the most expensive of all spices, is available in strands or ground form. It is made from the dried stamens of the crocus flower. The quality of this spice varies greatly.

SEA SCALLOPS: we used sea scallops with the coral (roe) attached.

SEMOLINA: a hard part of the wheat which is sifted out and used mainly for making pasta.

SWISS CHARD: remove coarse white stems, wash leaves thoroughly, cook leaves as individual recipes indicate.

SUGAR: we used coarse granulated table sugar unless otherwise specified.

Confectioners': also known as powdered sugar.

VANILLA EXTRACT: we used imitation vanilla extract.

VINEGAR: we used both white and brown (malt) vinegar in this book.

Red wine: made from red wine, often flavored with herbs and spices.

White wine: made from white wine, often flavored with herbs and spices.

WINE: we used good quality red and white wines.

YEAST: allow 2 teaspoons (¼oz) dry active yeast to each ½oz fresh yeast.

CUP AND SPOON MEASURES

To ensure accuracy in your recipes use standard metric measuring equipment.

(a) 8oz fluid cup for measuring liquids.
(b) a graduated set of four cups – measuring 1 cup, half, third and quarter cup – for items such as flour, sugar, etc. When measuring in these fractional cups, level off at the brim.
(c) a graduated set of five spoons: tablespoon (½ fluid oz liquid capacity), teaspoon, half, quarter and eighth teaspoons.

All our spoon measurements are level.

We have used large eggs with an average weight of 2oz each in all recipes.

INDEX

Story June, 86
from WIB

MAKE YOUR OWN BROTH

CHICKEN BROTH
4lb chicken bones
2 onions, chopped
2 stalks celery, chopped
2 carrots, chopped
3 bay leaves
2 teaspoons black peppercorns
20 cups water

Combine all ingredients in large pan, simmer, uncovered, 2 hours; strain.

Makes about 10 cups.
■ Broth can be made 4 days ahead.
■ Storage: Covered, in refrigerator.
■ Freeze: Suitable.
■ Microwave: Not suitable.

VEGETABLE BROTH
1 large carrot, chopped
1 large parsnip, chopped
2 onions, chopped
6 stalks celery, chopped
4 bay leaves
2 teaspoons black peppercorns
12 cups water

Combine all ingredients in large pan, simmer, uncovered, 1½ hours; strain.

Makes about 5 cups.
■ Broth can be made 4 days ahead.
■ Storage: Covered, in refrigerator.
■ Freeze: Suitable.
■ Microwave: Not suitable.

FISH BROTH
3lb fish bones
12 cups water
1 onion, chopped
2 stalks celery, chopped
2 bay leaves
1 teaspoon black peppercorns

Combine all ingredients in large pan, simmer, uncovered, 2 hours; strain.

Makes about 10 cups.
■ Broth can be made 4 days ahead.
■ Storage: Covered, in refrigerator.
■ Freeze: Suitable.
■ Microwave: Not suitable.

BEEF BROTH
4lb meaty beef bones
2 onions
2 stalks celery, chopped
2 carrots, chopped
3 bay leaves
2 teaspoons black peppercorns
20 cups water
12 cups water, extra

Place bones and unpeeled chopped onions in roasting pan. Bake, uncovered, in 400˚F oven about 1 hour or until bones and onions are well browned. Transfer bones and onions to large pan, add celery, carrots, bay leaves, peppercorns and water, simmer, uncovered, 3 hours. Add extra water, simmer, uncovered, further 1 hour; strain.

Makes about 10 cups.
■ Broth can be made 4 days ahead.
■ Storage: Covered, in refrigerator.
■ Freeze: Suitable.
■ Microwave: Not suitable.

Salads

Sensational recipes for all occasions

COUNTRY COOKING

Healthy Heart Cookbook

VEGETARIAN COOKING

THE BEST **SEAFOOD** RECIPES

Italian COOKING CLASS COOKBOOK

CHICKEN COOKBOOK

PLUS duck, quail, turkey, goose and more

PASTA COOKBOOK

More than 170 recipes

CHINESE COOKING CLASS COOKBOOK

STARTERS AND SOUPS

BEGINNERS' COOKBOOK

FINGER FOOD

Best ever party food
Tempting hot and cold savouries
Do ahead and freezing tips